RELIGION AND SOCIETY

RELIGION AND SOCIETY

Debiprasad Chattopadhyaya

Religion and Society
Debiprasad Chattopadhyaya

First Published by Ma-Le Prakashana, Bangalore, 1987
First Aakar Edition 2013
Reprinted 2020
Reprinted 2024

ISBN 978-93-5002-251-1 (Pb)

Published by
AAKAR BOOKS
28 E Pocket IV, Mayur Vihar Phase I
Delhi 110 091, India
www.aakarbooks.com

Printed at
D.K. Fine Art Press, Delhi

Aid to the Reader

Notes and References

The references in the footnotes are to the works given in the Bibliography. Where only one book by an author is included in the Bibliography only his name occurs in the footnote; where more than one work by the same author is included in the Bibliography, the name of the author is followed by the initials of the title of the work in Roman capitals. Contributions to journals and general reference works are indicated by the word 'in' preceding these.

Aakar Books is grateful to

Dr. Debiprasad Chattopadhyaya's daughters Aditi and Atashi for giving us the opportunity and privilege of publishing this book.

Calcutta University for according the necessary permission to publish the book.

Dr. G. Ramakrishna for his interest in the publication of this work.

K.K. Saxena

Contents

Contents

Introduction

The present work comprises the "Stephanos Nirmalendu Ghose Lectures for 1981" of the Calcutta University, which I had the honour to deliver at the auditorium of the National Library, Calcutta, in July 1986. I must at once thank Dr. Ashim Dasgupta, Director of the National Library, not only for providing me with all the facilities for delivering the lectures but also for taking personal interest in these to the extent of listening to me. I am also extremely grateful to Professor A.W. Mahmud for inaugurating the lectures and introducing me to the audience with kind words about me and my work, perhaps prompted more by his personal affection for me than my intrinsic worth. Dr. Santosh Kumar Mukherjee, Deputy Registrar (Estates and Trusts) of the Calcutta University spared himself of no drudgery for organising the lectures and to obtain from the University authorities the permission to get the lectures published in book-form by some publisher of my choice. I cannot really thank him enough.

*   *   *   *

The lectures as delivered are not published here in exactly the same form. Besides some alterations I eventually felt necessary in many places, the stipulated time for each lecture obliged me to shorten its length considerably. In the present book, however, I had the opportunity to use the lectures as drafted in full. This has enabled me to explain certain points more fully than I was able to do in the lectures as delivered.

In the present introduction, however, I shall try to discuss specially one point which, though related to the main theme of the lectures, could hardly be included in the lectures as planned.

* * * *

Rai Bahadur G.C. Ghosh, on whose funding the lectureship is instituted by the University, was clear and categorical about one point. He was honestly convinced that everything good and noble about man is derived from divine sources and hence embodied in religion. He therefore intended the present series of lectures to be a defence—or, perhaps more appropriately, to be a propagation of religion. I shall return to this basic question in the concluding portion of the present book, where I hope to discuss and also to review the contemporary world situation. In the Introduction, however, I shall try to emphasise another point. Rai Bahadur G.C. Ghosh was inclined also to believe that the noblest values of religion were most vividly expressed in Christianity. In short, he was also himself a devout Christian. Accordingly—besides perpetuating the memory of his son who died young and in whose name the lectureship is instituted—he was also motivated by the desire to propagate the noble values he was inclined to believe as embodied in Christianity. In the *Calendar of the University of Calcutta for 1956*, we read longish correspondences the donor had with the University authorities from August 1919 to November 1939 though, curiously enough, the first series of the lectures was already delivered in 1921 by Professor A.A. Macdonell. It is hard to guess from the *Calendar* why, even after the lectureship was already under progress, the donor wanted to be more specific about the subject-matter he desired to be highlighted. In any case, we read in the *Calendar* the following letter written by him to the University on September 24, 1924 and as modified on the suggestion of the Syndicate on November 29, 1939:

> Christ is one of the high manifestations of God. So the highest conception of God in the mind of man is Christ. So if man would lift up Christ in him, his spirit would enable him to live his life, expressed in loving service and sacrifice for fellowmen,

his highest advancement and greatest happiness would be attained in the end.

We have added emphasis to the above, because the donor comes out here rather passionately as a devout Christian. What he says about Christ has been shared indeed by honest pious Christians for centuries. But things are somewhat different with honest historians when they look back at the historical Christ or Jesus of Nazareth and at early Christianity, i.e. as contrasted with the form it assumed from the time of Constantine, when it became a highly organised state religion. However, the point that I shall try to show here may sound strange to many. The expressions used by G.C. Ghosh—"if man would lift up Christ in him, his spirit would enable him to live his life, expressed in loving service and sacrifice," etc.—should remain acceptable to the honest historians, inclusive of the class-conscious revolutionary ones, though the sense in which Ghosh apparently wanted these to be understood is in need of very serious modification.

Thus modified, early Christianity appears to have been an organised revolutionary movement, aiming above all to emancipate the oppressed and exploited classes and its leader—the historical Christ—was tortured and killed by the ruling class because he was leading an armed uprising against the exploiting class. There is thus a good deal of real sense even for a contemporary communist to "lift up Christ in him", so that the essence of his teachings may acquire real truth instead of repeating only empty words concerning "loving service and sacrifice for fellowmen".

I shall try to show this by following mainly the writings of Frederick Engels, Archibald Robertson and Barrows Dunham. Their points, lying as these do under a huge heap of theology accumulated for centuries, would appear to many as outrageously absurd. The safer course for me would, therefore, be to allow these writers to speak for themselves.

Engels begins with what he calls "the German criticism of the Bible" specially by Bruno Bauer (1809-1882), whose scathing criticism of the Gospels and Epistles, according to

Engels, perhaps went too far, but who nevertheless did great service towards the demystification of the Bible:

> His greatest service consists not merely in having made a pitiless criticism of the Gospels and the Epistles of the apostles, but in having for the first time seriously undertaken an inquiry into not only the Jewish and Greco-Alexandrian elements but the purely Greek and Greco-Roman elements that first opened for Christianity the career of a universal religion. The legend that Christianity arose ready and complete out of Judaism and, starting from Palestine, conquered the world with its dogma already defined in the main and its morals, has been untenable since Bruno Bauer; it can continue to vegetate only in the theological faculties and with people who wish 'to keep religion alive for the people' even at the expense of science. The enormous influence which the Philonic school of Alexandria and Greco-Roman vulgar philosophy—platonic and mainly Stoic—had on Christianity, which became the state religion under Constantine, is far from having been defined in detail, but its existence has been proved and that is primarily the achievement of Bruno Bauer: he laid the foundation of the proof that Christianity was not imported from outside—from Judea—into the Romano-Greek world and imposed on it, but that, at least in its world-religion form, it is that world's own product. Bauer, of course, like all those who are fighting against deep-rooted prejudices, overreached his aim in this work. In order to define through literary sources, too, Philo's and particularly Seneca's influence on emerging Christianity and to show up the authors of the New Testament formally as downright plagiarists of those philosophers, he had to place the appearance of the new religion about half a century later, to reject the opposing accounts of Roman historians and take extensive liberties with historiography in general. According to him Christianity as such appears only under the Flavians, the literature of the New Testament only under Hadrian, Antoninus and Marcus Aurelius. As a result the New Testament accounts of Jesus and his disciples are deprived for Bauer of any historical background: they are diluted in legends in which the phases of interior development and the moral struggles of the first communities are transferred to more or

> less fictitious persons. Not Galilee and Jerusalem, but Alexandria and Rome, according to Bauer, are the birth- places of the New religion.[1]

In spite of the exaggerations of Bauer, his demystification of the Christian scripture proved for Engels the opening of new understanding of early Christianity. We shall first quote extensively from Engels and then return to further researches from the Marxist viewpoint of the subject, specially as carried forward by Archibald Robertson and Barrows Dunham. Engels observes:

"The history of early Christianity has notable points in common with the modern working-class movement. Like the latter, Christianity was originally a movement of oppressed people: it first appeared as the religion of slaves and emancipated slaves, of poor people deprived of all rights, of peoples subjugated or dispersed by Rome. Both Christianity and the workers' socialism preach forthcoming salvation from bondage and misery; Christianity places this salvation in a life beyond, after death, in heaven; socialism places it in this world, in a transformation of society. Both are persecuted and baited, their adherents are despised and made the objects of exclusive laws, the former as enemies of the human race, the latter as enemies of the state, enemies of religion, the family, and social order. And in spite of all persecution, nay, even spurred on by it, they forge victoriously, irresistibly ahead....

"The parallel between the two historical phenomena forces itself upon our attention as early as the Middle Ages in the first risings of the oppressed peasants and particularly of the town plebeians. These risings, like all mass movements of the Middle Ages, were bound to wear the mask of religion and appeared as the restoration of early Christianity from spreading degeneration; but behind the religious exaltation there were every time very tangible worldly interests. This appeared most splendidly in the organisation of the Bohemian Taborites under Jan Zizka, of glorious memory; But this trait pervades the whole of the Middle Ages till it gradually fades away after the German Peasant War to revive again with the working-men Communists after 1830. The French revolutionary Communists, as also in particular Weitling and his supporters, referred to early Christianity long before Ernest Renan's words: 'If I wanted to give you an idea of the early Christian communities I would tell you to look at a local section of the International Working Men's Association.'"[2]

Further: "We therefore see that the Christianity of that time, which was still unaware of itself, was as different as heaven from earth from the later dogmatically fixed world religion of the Council of Nicene; one cannot be recognised in the other. Here we have neither the dogma nor the morals of later Christianity but instead a feeling that one is struggling against the whole world and that the struggle will be a victorious one; an eagerness for the struggle and a certainty of victory which are totally lacking in Christians of today and which are to be found in our time only at the other pole of society, among the socialists.

"In fact, the struggle against a world that at the beginning was superior in force, and at the same time of the innovators among themselves, is common to the early Christians and the socialists. Neither of these two great movements was made by leaders or prophets—although there are prophets enough among both of them—they are mass movements."[3]

And who were the persons whom we meet in early Christianity struggling against the whole world? Here also Engels is inclined to see similarity between early Christianity and modern Communism:

"What kind of people were the first Christians recruited from? Mainly from the 'labouring and burdened', the members of the lowest strata of the people, as becomes a revolutionary element. And what did they consist of? In the towns of impoverished free men, all sorts of people, like the 'mean whites' of the southern slave states and the European beach-combers and adventurers in colonial and Chinese seaports, then of emancipated slaves and, above all, actual slaves: on the large estates in Italy, Sicily, and Africa of slaves, and in the rural districts of the provinces of small peasants who had fallen more and more into bondage through debt."[4]

It is thus that further studies in early Christianity from the Marxist point of view takes a new turn as it were. One of the most notable books embodying it is *The Origins of Christianity* by Archibald Robertson (London 1953). Reexamining a vast mass of materials which contain often very clear though sometimes comparatively subtle indications, and critically scaling off the frequent tendency of later amendments and alterations sought to be introduced into the Bible evidently intended to soften down the radical implications of early Christianity, he arrives at the view that the historical Jesus was so brutally killed because of the simple reason that he, after John the Baptist, was actively organising an armed insurrection of the oppressed people against the oppressors. The book requires to be read and perhaps also reread—by those honestly interested in knowing the historical Christ and his actual message, though unfortunately we do not have the scope here to reiterate all—or even the major—evidences on the basis of which the author convincingly substantiates his views. It is essential for our purpose at least to quote the author's own summing up of the view itself. As he puts it, "the earliest parts of the Gospels—proved to be such by internal evidence and by a comparative study of the Synoptics—point back to a revolutionary movement led first by John the Baptist and then by Jesus the Nazoraean, and aimed at the overthrow of Roman and Herodian rule in Palestine and the establishment of an earthly 'kingdom of God' in which the first would be last and the last first, the rich sent empty away and the poor filled with good things and given houses and land. The followers of John and Jesus were called Notzrim or Nazoraeans, not from the village of Nazareth, but from the Hebrew word *natzar*, "to keep"—...as keepers of secrets...

"The Nazoraeans were probably an offshoot of the Essenes. The Essenes, says Josephus, 'are despisers of riches...

Nor is there anyone to be found among them who has more than another; for it is a law among them that those who come to them must let what they have be common to the whole order... So there is, as it were, one patrimony among all the brethren'...

"The movement of John the Baptist was nipped in the bud by Antipas. A Nazoraean attempt to seize Jerusalem led to the crucifixion of Jesus by Pilate. According to the Synoptics, Jesus was believed by some to be John the Baptist risen from death, and by others to be Elijah or one of the ancient prophets. The whole history of the Messianic idea from Daniel onwards shows that it was the projection of the hopes of a revolutionary movement which had taken root among simple and ignorant people, attaching itself to leader after leader and able to survive the death of many such. We need not wonder that it survived the death of Jesus..."[5]

Fully acknowledging his basic indebtedness to Archibald Robertson's book, Barrows Dunham, in his *Heroes and Heretics* (New York, 1967) carries forward this new approach to the understanding of Christ. As he sums up his main point:

"Let me say at once, then, that I believe the historical Jesus to have been the leader of an armed movement for national liberation. The movement, betrayed on the eve of insurrection, was crushed, and the leader was executed. These events happened in perhaps, A.D. 30—at any rate, before Pontius Pilate's recall to Rome in the year 36.

"I am aware that it may seem alarming, and even horrifying, to think of Jesus as an active revolutionist. There is in the Gospels, however, some direct evidence for this view—evidence which is the stronger because it cannot be suspected of tendentiousness and may therefore be thought to record a tradition of fact. "[6]

The selected data on which the view is based requires to be understood in depth, bearing in mind that the Biblical passages quoted by him are from the translation of the *New English Bible* (Oxford and Cambridge University Presses, 1961). As Dunham says:

"Let us now examine the evidence for this view. We have said that the evangelists have left traces of original facts, rather like geological remnants which show what the ancient topography was. For example:

"'Ever since the coming of John the Baptist the kingdom of Heaven has been subjected to violence and violent men are seizing it.' Again, a parallel passage in Luke:

'Until John, it was the Law and the prophets: since then, there is the good news of the kingdom of God, and everyone forces his way in.'

"These are strange passages to find in narratives that purport to describe a man of non-revolutionary aims and other-worldly intentions...

"My guess is that the passages assert a fact which a thousand years of experience had demonstrated—namely, that the liberation of the country required armed effort, and that thus only could one attain 'the kingdom of God.'

"Further, Luke's Gospel has a remarkable twenty-second chapter, in which among passages apparently put in later to validate the Eucharist, we get the picture of a band of revolutionaries, a sort of executive committee or general staff, supping together on the eve of insurrection. The leader announces, what he has surmised or been told, that one of them is a police agent.....

"Then, suddenly, the leader says,

'When I sent you out barefoot without purse or pack, were you ever short of anything?' 'No,' they answered. 'It is different now,' he said: 'whoever has a purse had better take it with him, and his pack too; and if he has no sword, let him sell his cloak to buy one. For scripture says, 'And he was counted among the outlaws, and these words, I tell you, must find fulfilment in me; indeed, all that is written of me is being fulfilled'. 'Look, Lord,' they said, 'we have two swords here.' 'Enough, enough!' he replied.

"It sounds like insurrection, does it not ? If that is what it was, then Judas's treason becomes for the first time intelligible. In the Gospels, his act of betrayal consists in identifying Jesus to the arresting officers. But neither they nor the Sanhedrin needed such help. Jesus was by that time a notable public figure, who had been greeted at the city gates by a throng shouting the insurrectionary cry *Ho-sanna!* (—'Deliver us.') But if Judas brought word that the insurrection was about to begin, that was news well worth thirty pieces of silver.

"Finally, that insurrection was the order of the day may be seen from two passages concerning Barabbas. Mark says (15:7), 'As it happened, the man known as Barabbas was then in custody with the rebels who had committed murder in the rising' (NEB). Luke says (23:19), 'This man had been put in prison for a rising that had taken place in the city, and for murder' (NEB). Those were tumultuous times, and only the rich were safely pro-Roman.

"If the historical Jesus was a social revolutionary, we can more readily appreciate the considerable body of radical doctrine which the Gospels contain. The Golden Rule suffices of itself to outlaw exploitation, but, besides this, there are many doctrines which envisage a precise reversal of the social order. The last are to be first; the lowly are to inherit the earth.

"Where the movement is concerned, there is to be no 'business as usual'—the money-changers are driven from the Temple. The upper class collaborators with Rome are 'whited sepulchres full of dead men's bones.' The legalists 'strain at (out) a gnat and swallow a camel.' On being asked a treacherous question whether the Roman tax ought to be paid, Jesus asks to see the sort of coin that usually serves for payment. One of his interlocutors produces a *denarius,* and then stands self-confuted, self- betrayed—for who would be so likely to have a *denarius* as a man in the pay of Roman officials?...

"Meanwhile the disciples, reminded of how much they have themselves given up, begin to worry about future rewards. According to Mark, the answer is: 'I tell you this: there is no one who has given up home; brothers or sisters, mother, father or children, or land, for my sake and for the

Gospel, who will not receive in this age a hundred times as much—houses, brothers and sisters, mothers and children, and land and persecutions besides; and in the age to come eternal life. But many who are first will be last and the last first.'

"In this age! The rewards, then, are not all transcendental and postponed to some other order of existence. Some of them, at least, are to be enjoyed in the same historical continuum in which they were striven for. These will consist in economic prosperity ('houses' and 'lands') and in a wider, more intimate brotherhood".....

"Lastly, there is no doubt that the movement had won the people. We have the priests' word for that: they told Pilate, 'His teaching is causing disaffection among the people all through Judaea. It started from Galilee and has spread as far as this city.' There is some reason to think, indeed, that the Romans and their collaborators struck at the last possible moment, and that further delay would have been perilous. For Jesus had understood the law of all such movements, that people must be enlightened about their true social interest and then organised to attain them: 'Ye shall know the truth, and the truth shall make you free.'"[7]

It is indeed tempting to quote more from Dunham's brilliant analysis of the evidences. Unfortunately, however, our scope is extremely limited.

But we should like to add that the message of armed uprising for the liberation of the oppressed did not end with the gruesome murder of Jesus. Here is a striking example of this. Thomas Munzer, the leader of the peasant war in Germany, while calling the princes of Saxony and the people to rise in arms against the Roman priests, gave the clarion call of an outright political agitator, using—as a pious Christian is only expected to do—the authority of Christ himself:

"Does not Christ say, 'I came not to send peace, but a sword? What must you (the princes of Saxony) do with that sword? Only one thing if you wish to be the servants of God, and that is to drive out and destroy the evil ones who stand in the way of the Gospel. Christ ordered very earnestly (Luke, 19: 27) 'bring hither mine enemies and slay them before me.' Do not give us any empty phrases that the power of God will do it without the aid of your sword, since then it would rust in its sheath.... Those who stand in the way of God's revelation must be destroyed mercilessly, as Hezekiah, Cyrus, Josiah, Daniel and Elias destroyed the priests of Baal, else the Christian Church will never come back to its source. We must uproot the weeds in God's vineyard at harvest time..... God said in the Fifth Book of Moses, [7], 'thou shalt not show mercy unto the idolators, but ye shall destroy their altars, and break down their images and burn them with fire that I shall not be wroth at you.'"[8]

* * * *

With these words about the new way of looking back at historical Jesus and the movement he led, we may return to the stipulation of the donor of the present lecturership. He observes: "If man would lift up Christ in him, his spirit would enable him to live his life expressed in loving service and sacrifice for fellowmen, his highest advancement and greatest happiness would be attained in the end." Whatever the donor might have had in his mind, we have only one point to add to this with the new understanding of the historical Christ, which is increasingly gaining grounds. From the viewpoint of the establishment all this is rather alarming to say, specially in these days of great social turmoil when, in spite of all the anxieties and grimness we are suffering from, we also hear the sound of suffering humanity knocking at the doors to be opened for global communism.

* * * *

In the lectures as delivered, however, I have not gone into the question of early Christianity. This is primarily because I felt that for the Indian audience, at any rate, the more important need is the reexamination of certain widespread notions about Indian religions in the general background of Indian history.

* * * *

It remains for me to add only one more point. The present book is not the first one I have written on Indian philosophy and religion. As a matter of fact, I have been writing on Indian philosophy and religion for the last three decades. Naturally enough, I cannot always have new things to say about the same subject. So I had often to repeat or reiterate some points discussed in my earlier works. Of these, I must specially mention the following, from which a considerable amount of material had to be taken and restated in the present book: *(1) Lokayata, (2) Indian Philosophy, (3) Indian Atheism, (4) What is Living and What is Dead in Indian Philosophy,* and *(5) Knowledge and Intervention.* However, as I do not expect any reader of my books to remember everything I have said in those books and, moreover, as what I have taken from these are placed in a new context, I do hope to have the indulgence allowed to say certain things I have said before.

REFERENCES

1. Engels in OR 321-2.
2. Ib. 313-15.
3. Ib. 326-7.
4. Ib. 330-31.
5. A. Robertson 93-96.
6. B. Dunham 51.
7. Ib. 53-7.
8. Quoted by Engels PWG 70.

1

Before Religion

I am profoundly grateful to the Vice-Chancellor of the University of Calcutta and his colleagues for giving me this opportunity—which indeed is also grand honour—of delivering the Stephanos Nirmalendu Ghose Lectures for the year 1981. At the same time it will be an obvious audacity on my part not to mention how diffident I feel to take the responsibility I am required to. I am fully aware of the fact that I had only been a somewhat timid teacher of philosophy compared to those who have delivered the same lectures before me. I find in the list of their names those of my own teachers like Nalini Kanta Brahma—to whom I literally owe my initiation in philosophy—and Surendra Nath Dasgupta and Sarvapalli Radhakrishnan, whose international reputation as historians and interpreters of Indian philosophy is hardly in need of any epithet. I also find in the list a few names of illustrious scholars and writers from abroad like those of A.A. Macdonell and Aldous Huxley, compared to whom my own stature is hardly of any significance. But I must not make my personal apologies too long, lest it be misconstrued as a reflection on the judicious selection of the Vice-Chancellor. I should rather proceed to discuss straight away what I am asked to.

1. 'Spirit of God in Man'

As is rather well-known, the subject intended to be covered by this lectureship is religion, or, as it is sometimes called, comparative religion. The letter of invitation I have received from the university mentions—evidently according to the desire of Rai Bahadur Ghosh on whose funding it is instituted—that "the lecturer will show that every religion is the product of the institution of the spirit of God within man." This, as I am inclined to understand, is true, though not the whole truth. Accordingly, I shall first try to show why this is true and then add a few words so that we may have some idea of the whole truth.

Obviously enough, belief in God—which, to put it in more theological terms, is the sense of the institution of the spirit of God within man—has been a necessary precondition for at least all the major organised religions in world history. Even Buddhism, which is sometimes mentioned as the perplexing phenomenon of "religion without God", is, in the ultimate analysis, not really an exception to this. Whatever might have been the original teachings of the Buddha—which, for all that we know, won the ears of a rather restricted band of followers and was presumably more in the nature of a socio-moral programme than religion as generally understood—had eventually to make room for a supreme God surrounded by a host of demigods, and only thus move towards being an organised religion in its full sense. The transformation had been momentous, so much so that it had to acquire a new name for itself, which was Mahāyāna. Perhaps to soothe an uneasy conscience, certain formalities of showing continuity with the alleged atheism of the Buddha could not be entirely done away with. Thus Nagarjuna—the great representative of Mahāyāna, if not its actual founder—professed to adduce certain theoretical considerations against the possible existence of God, as is suggested by the title *Iśvara-kartṛtva-nirākaraṇa-viṣṇoḥ- ekakartṛtva-nirākaraṇa*, a work attributed to him and surviving for us in the vast Tibetan collection called the Tanjur (bsTan-'gyur).[1] A critical survey of the book, however, shows that it is in fact not intended to reject the supreme God of Mahāyāna Buddhism—usually called Avalokitesvara, for whom

Nagarjuna is said to have had the most profound reverence. It is more in the nature of a philosophical refutation of the concept of causality as such and hence by implication also of the view of the world ever being created or coming into existence—a theoretical position required by the Śūnyavāda of Nagarjuna. In any case, notwithstanding such sporadic[2] philosophical formalities giving us the apparent impression that Mahayana retained the spirit of the original atheism of the Buddha, the fact remains that with the eventual development of Buddhism into the Mahayana so-called, God makes room for Himself in a big way, leaving undisturbed what is called in theological terminology "the spirit of God within man", taken of course not in the absolute ontological sense but in the more popular sense of the belief in God being an essential characteristic of all organised religions.

I have mentioned all this only to emphasise one point. The stipulation, namely that the lecturer will have to show that the institution of the spirit of God in man remains inescapably true from the historical viewpoint, despite the often-mentioned example of Buddhism having been a religion without God. In other words, there is hardly any scope to raise any doubt concerning the historical truth contained in the stipulation.

It is different, however, when it comes to the question of the whole truth. For this purpose one has to raise the further question concerning the very *making of the sense of God in man*, or, when such a sense is taken as an essential characteristic of religion, the question concerning the *making of religion itself*. This point—the addition proposed to have the whole truth—is important. First, ethnological researches correlated to archaeology want us to accept as a fact that there was a time when human beings had no notion of God and hence of the spirit thereof. Secondly, in one view at any rate—which, incidentally, in spite of provoking as much hope as hostility in the world today, is acquiring an ever-increasing importance—it is possible to foresee a future when men are going to do without any God, and hence of His spirit within.

Thus in short, in order to have the whole truth we have to reformulate the point and assert that though the institutions of the spirit of God in man had indeed been an essential feature of all organised religions, religion itself—along with all its concomitants—had a definite beginning, as definite again as it is going to have an end. The whole thing came into being, as it is going to pass away. If we ignore this we are left at best with wearisome theology, which had indeed a long innings for centuries, but not the hard core of what happened in history.

All this, I am at once anxious to add, is not intended to be a historical *evaluation* of religion. Though transitory after all, religion had an enormously complicated role in human history. Without its making, the very making of civilisation is not easily conceivable—a point which, as we shall see in the next lecture, has been brilliantly analysed by Gordon Childe. During the career of human civilisation, again, its role had often been most complex and contradictory—ranging from being an instrument for enforcing abject submission of the toiling masses to that of inspiring the revolt against tyranny and oppression, as was the case in early Christianity. In this medley of assorted functions of religion, one point is in need of special emphasis. Throughout the career of civilisations so far, it had in fact been a historical necessity. The career of the human beings began with a struggle against nature: men have progressively acquired the knowledge and capacity to control the forces of nature and extract from nature wealth for the satisfaction of human needs. This eventually led them to the threshold of civilisation, when emerged a new problem, namely the need for the regulations necessary in order to adjust the relations of men to one another and especially the distribution of the available wealth. At this stage, a section of the community itself could serve the function as custodians of the wealth in relation to another section, and when this section soon converted itself into the owners thereof, the product of the labour of others could be appropriated by it for its own satisfaction. It thus no longer remained the simple struggle of man against nature; to this was added another form of struggle, namely that of man against man. In short, human community was split into a privileged minority and an under privileged majority—the knowledge and power over nature going mainly in favour of the former. The impoverished masses—who in the earlier phase of civilisation were simply slaves and who in its advanced phase became the propertyless working class—were henceforth confronted with a dual uncertainty and a dual misery: those coming from the still uncontrolled nature and those coming from the exploitative machinery of the ruling class. Science and technology was left with the task of progressively delimiting the former, while religion to blunt the sense of the latter. From the historical point of view this was a necessity, for without the accumulation of wealth in the hands of the ruling minority, the spectacular achievements of civilisation so far could hardly be possible. At the same time, this made life for the masses too painful or too full of sufferings and uncertainties to be borne without some form of palliative remedy. This was supplied by religion—the belief in God who alone could assure justice, if not right now at least sometimes later, if not in this world at least in the after-world. This had gone on throughout the career of civilisation till recent times, when the knowledge of and power over nature have reached such magnificent dimensions that the concentration of wealth in the hands of the privileged minority, far from remaining a precondition for further human progress, has actually become a fetter for it. In short, conditions are created in the contemporary context for the basic restructuring of society, which can do away with the palliative remedy for miseries resulting from split-society—a historical necessity so far.

All this accounts for the fact that no amount of atheistic propaganda and no amount of philosophical criticisms could by themselves uproot the religious beliefs from the minds of the masses. Theology may add a certain amount of halo to religion but does not sustain it. Philosophy can expose its inner inconsistencies and lack of logic, but cannot uproot it. It draws its nourishment from some concrete material conditions, which, so long as they are allowed to persist, will have religion itself unaffected. That is why Karl Marx, when he was taking the first decisive step to Marxism, parted company with the 'Young Hegelians' who were spending all their energies in the philosophical criticism of religion. And he observed:

> *Religious* distress is at the same time the *expression* of real distress and the *protest* against real distress. Religion is the sigh of the oppressed creature, the heart of a heartless world, just as it is the spirit of a spiritless situation. It is the *opium* of the people.
>
> The abolition of religion as the *illusory* happiness of the people is required for their *real* happiness. The demand to give up the illusions about its condition is the *demand to give up a condition which needs illusions*. The criticism of religion is therefore *in embryo the criticism of the vale of woe*, the *halo* of which is religion......
>
> *The task of history*, therefore, once the *world beyond the truth* has disappeared, is to establish the *truth of this world*. The immediate *task of philosophy* which is at the service of history, once the *saintly form* of self-alienation has been unmasked, is to unmask self-alienation in its *unholy forms*. Thus the criticism of heaven turns into the criticism of the earth, the *criticism of religions* into the *criticism of right* and the *criticism of theology* into the *criticism of politics*.[3]

Such an attitude, as is rather well-known, eventually leads Marx to reformulate the basic task of philosophy in a totally different way: "The philosophers have only *interpreted* the world in various ways; the point, however, is to *change* it". Indeed, if philosophical thoughts are ultimately rooted in material conditions, how can there be a really radical change in it without changing the material conditions themselves? His view of religion is only an extension of this point to philosophical questions, as is evident from what has just been quoted.

Marx's view of religion is frequently distorted, wilfully or otherwise. Our purpose, however, is to try to review it as fully and clearly as we can. Only thus can we hope to understand why the sense of God in man had a definite beginning as it is destined also to have a definite end.

2. Three Basic Stages of Social Evolution

Since religion is inconceivable without man and man inconceivable without society, the starting point of our understanding of religion as viewed in Marxism is an idea of the evolution of society. We quote George Thomson for a brief account of it, if for no other reason than its piercing clarity combined with the most admirable absorption of the fundamentals of Marxism. Thomson observes:

> The evolution of human society has gone far enough for us to identify three main stages, corresponding to successive advances in the mode of production: pre-class society, class society, and the classless society of the future.
>
> In pre-class society, or primitive communism, the level of production was so low that the maximum effort of the whole community was absorbed in maintaining it at the minimum level of subsistence. There was no surplus. It was impossible for one man to live on the labour of another. There were no economic inequalities, and no social inequalities except the prestige earned by individual merit.
>
> When the technique of production had advanced far enough to leave a surplus over and above the immediate needs of the community, it became possible for different groups to specialise in different crafts, while the rest of the community supplied them food. Such divisions of labour, as they are called, led to further improvements in technique, till eventually there emerged a new division of labour—qualitatively new—a division between the actual producers and the organisers of production. The organisers of production were the chiefs or priests, the pioneers of such sciences as astronomy and mathematics, which were necessary for the development of agriculture. The nature of their work was such as to place them in a position of authority, and in time these custodians of the

> means of production converted themselves into owners. The community was divided into a working class and a ruling class. So we see that class society was brought into being by advances in the mode of production. The same is true of the successive phases of class society. Capitalism, in particular, has raised the productivity of labour to a level so high that the division of society into classes has now become an obstacle to the further development of the productive forces. Hence our modern paradox of poverty in the midst of plenty. In striving to maintain the rate of profit, the capitalist class, which is controlled by a few handful of big monopolists, is compelled to reduce wages, with the result that the workers, who form the overwhelming majority of the earth's inhabitants, are unable to buy the goods they produce. To this conflict there is only one solution—the socialist revolution. Having destroyed the capitalist state, the workers must create a new form of state power which will enable them to take over the means of production and thus abolish the system of private profit. When that has been done, the result is, as we know from the history of the Soviet Union, that production increases, uninterrupted by slumps, and at the same time, thanks to a fully planned economy, there is a continual rise in the people's standard of living. The conflict is resolved by abolishing the exploitation of man by man, and so the necessary conditions are created for the new communism, the classless society of the future.[4]

The account being very brief could touch some points only cryptically and hence there is a need for more elaboration. From the viewpoint of our present discussion, one of these is that of the transition from primitive pre-class society to class society, because, as we are going to see, it is directly connected with the making of religion. We shall return to the question of the making of religion in our next lecture where we shall have the advantage of being guided by one of the greatest archaeologists, V. Gordon Childe, who has shown why for the very making of human civilisation, the making of religion had been a historical necessity, whatever might have been the other consequences of it. For the present let us have a few other clarifications about the passage just quoted.

Put in the terminologies of Hegelian logic—to which Marx and Engels were profoundly indebted—the outlines of social evolution sketched above illustrate the fundamental laws of dialectics, namely "the negation of the negation". The primitive pre-class society is negated by class society, while class society in its turn is negated by the classless society of the future. Moreover, this process of the negation of the negation leads to something qualitatively new, for the classless society of the future, though in some sense is a return to some features of primitive pre-class society of the past, is a return to it in an incomparably higher level and hence to something qualitatively new. It is not a return to the conditions of the savages and early barbarians, where everybody is equal because of being equally poor, acquiring from nature with their rudimentary technology just enough to keep themselves alive or perishing when even that is not possible. On the contrary, it is moving forward to the stage in which everybody is equal because of being equally free from want and avoidable sufferings, thanks to the spectacular technological accomplishments man has in the meanwhile achieved and is progressively achieving. As the American lawyer-anthropologist L.H. Morgan, to whose researches Marx and Engels were basically indebted for the first full knowledge of the primitive pre-class society, observed: "Democracy in government, brotherhood in society, equality in rights and privileges and universal education foreshadow the next higher plane of society to which experience, intelligence and knowledge are steadily tending. *It will be a revival, in a higher form, of the liberty, equality and fraternity of the ancient gentes.*"[5]

Incidentally it may be mentioned here that Morgan, whose researches in primitive society went so much to the full formation of the dialectics of social evolution of Marx and Engels, wanted to remain true to Christian piety. He submitted the proofs of the *Ancient Society*, his *magnum opus*, to Rev. J.H. McLennan, with a request for deleting from it anything that could be viewed as incompatible with the Old

Testament, but who was foolish enough to congratulate Morgan for adducing "the strongest arguments against the Darwinians."[6] Nor had Hegel anything to do with materialism, whose dialectics went so much to the shaping of Marxism. The law of the negation of the negation was for Hegel only the mode of self-expression of God or Absolute, for whom Hegel was pleased to have various terminological alternatives—Spirit, Thought, Idea, Notion, etc. But the dialectics of social evolution in Marxism scraps all these in favour of the materialist standpoint. The real force that worked for the negation of the pre-class society by class society and which is going to work again for the negation of class society by classless society is technological development or development of the mode of production. It is this that gives the Marxist view of the dialectics of social evolution a real footing on earth or makes it an account of what really happened in history, shorn of fancy or phantasy.

What follows from all this is another proposition exceedingly important for our own discussion. It is concerning the life-span of class society in absolute time-scale.

Notwithstanding the grave anxiety we are having today—when researches in thermo-nuclear power and biology leave men with the alternatives of omnicide or welfare hitherto undreamt of—the normal expectation of human survival on the earth is for an immeasurably long period. Hence also of that of the classless society dawning before us. When we look back at the past, we have a somewhat similar impression: in absolute time-scale the total period covered by the primitive pre-class society is immeasurably longer than that of the class society. In a rough estimate, as Gordon Childe has shown, the latter "as at best one hundredth part of the time during which men have been active on our planet."[7]

Thus, compared to the primitive pre-class society behind us, and compared to the classless society the prospect for which is brightening in spite of the present gloom, the career of class society is somewhat insignificant, enormously complicated though our present problem is of moving forward to the classless society. L.H. Morgan already noted this in his own way: "The time which has passed away since civilisation began is but a fragment of the past duration of man's existence; and but a fragment of the ages yet to come. The dissolution of society bids fair to become the termination of a career of which property is the end and aim: because such a career contains the elements of self-destruction."[8]

From the point of view of what we propose to discuss, i.e. the phenomenon called religion, this transitoriness of class society is of material importance. The making of religion is a necessary concomitant to the making of the class society, just as with the withering away of class society religion also is going to wither away, perhaps slowly rather than dramatically or at one stroke. In short, the essential transitoriness of class society is also indicative of the transitoriness of religion, howsoever complex might have been the career of religion during the rather brief period of its history in absolute time-scale.

3. Before Religion

The first question that requires to be answered in this connection is that before the splitting of society into antagonistic classes, had there actually been the phenomenon called religon, the essential preconditions of which are the belief in God, prayers and sacrifices to whom is beneficial not only from the viewpoint of our own spiritual upliftment but also—at least in popular understanding—from the viewpoint of fulfilling our desires? The question is answered by anthropology, supplemented where possible by archaeology. And the answer is in the negative. The real savages still surviving in certain pockets of the world, i.e. insofar as they are not penetrated by the missionaries and merchants—and hence not contaminated by ideas and attitudes alien to what is inherent of their own—are not aware of any God and have no practice of prayers, propitiations or sacrifices. "Similarly, wherever we can penetrate the prehistory of civilised peoples, we reach a level at which again there are no gods, no prayer or sacrifice."[9]

What then do they do when confronted with a hostile nature, against which they have to struggle for their survival? Jane Harrison has answered the question:

> The savage is a man of action. Instead of asking a god to do what he wants done, he does it or tries to do it himself; instead of prayers he utters spells. In a word, he practises magic, and above all he is strenuously and frequently engaged in dancing magical dances. When a savage wants sun or wind or rain, he does not go to church and prostrate himself before a false god; he summons his tribe and dances a sun dance or a wind dance or a rain dance. When he would hunt and catch a bear, he does not pray to his god for strength to outwit and outmatch the bear, he rehearses his hunt in a bear dance.[10]

Jane Harrison has used the word "magic" as contrasted with religion, and that as the characteristic peculiarity of the theory and practice of the primitive peoples. What, then, is magic?

> Magic rests on the principle that by creating the illusion that you control reality you can actually control it. In its initial stages it is simply mimetic. You want rain, so you perform a dance in which you mimic the gathering clouds, the thunderclap, and the falling shower. You enact in fantasy the fulfilment of the desired reality. In its later stages the mimetic act may be accompanied by a command, an imperative 'Rain!' But it is a command, not a request. This principle of collective compulsion corresponds to a stage of society at which the community is still an undivided whole, supreme over each and all of its members, presenting a weak but united front against the hostile world of nature.[11]

Such a technique of confronting the hostile nature is illusory indeed. But though illusory, it is not entirely futile. In a sense, it can and does supplement the real technique. There is, in other words, a positive aspect of it, from the viewpoint of which Frazer's characterisation of it as the precursor of science seems to make sense. Here is how George Thomson gives us a picturesque description of this aspect of magic.

> The Maoris have a potato dance. The young crop is liable to be blasted by east winds, so the girls go into the fields and dance, simulating with their bodies the rush of wind and rain and the sprouting and blossoming of the crops and as they dance they sing, calling on the crop to follow their example. They enact in fantasy the fulfilment of the desired reality. That is magic, an illusory technique supplementary to the real technique. But though illusory it is not futile. The dance cannot have any direct effect on the potatoes, but it can and does have an appreciable effect on the girls themselves. Inspired by the dance in the belief that it will save the crop, they proceed to the task of tending it with greater confidence and so with greater energy than before. And so it does have an effect on the crop after all. It changes their subjective attitude to reality, and so indirectly it changes reality.[12]

The efficacy of magic is thus psychological. But it is not a matter of individual psychology. As Jane Harrison continues:

> One element in the rite we have already observed, and that is, that it be done collectively, by a number of persons feeling the same emotion.... Collectivity and emotional tension, two elements that tend to turn the simple reaction into a rite, are—specially among primitive peoples—closely associated, indeed scarcely separable. The high emotional tension is to him only caused and maintained by a thing felt socially; it is what the tribe feels that is sacred, that is matter for ritual.... Intensity, then and collectivity go together....[13]

But this primitive collectivity is undermined by the advance in productive technique: it creates surplus and hence also the possibility of a few to live on the labour of many. This, as we are going to discuss in the next lecture, constitutes the material conditions for the point of departure from magic to religion. For the present, however, we shall have a few more words on magic—the ideology characteristic of the primitive pre-class society. Notwithstanding the advance in the productive technique, the belief in the efficacy of magic does not immediately vanish. It survives in folk culture or the culture of the downtrodden people, specially among the female folk of the backward peasants.

There is nothing strange about it. Primitive practices rendered obsolete by economic progress often find sanctuary in folk culture, "which is of interest to the historian just because it is a stratified repository of discarded practices and discarded beliefs. Long after men have ceased in normal life to do as their forefathers did, they cling to the belief that their prosperity depends in some way on the good-will of their ancestors."[14]

So the pre-religious magic survives even in the otherwise religious climate. An example of this is what is called *Vrata* in Bengal.

We are indebted to Abanindranath Tagore[15] for his remarkable monograph (in Bengali) on the *Vrata*-s *of Bengal.* We shall broadly follow here his treatment of the subject, avoiding it only on points where his idealist preoccupations have obscured the subject.

The nucleus of a *Vrata,* he observes, is a desire. Clustering round it are rhyme, riddle, song, dance and even pictorial representations called the *Alpanas*. All these are meant to represent the desire as if it were already fulfilled. As Abanindranath has put it:

'A *Vrata* is just a desire. We see it represented in the pictures, listen to its echo in the songs and the rhymes, witness its reactions in the dramas and dances; in short, the *Vrata*-s are but desires as sung, the painted desires, desires as moving and living.'

All this is clearly magic. That is, it would be a mistake to call them religion. Abanindranath has repeatedly said that the *Vrata*-s are neither prayers not propitiations. The attitude underlying the performance of a *Vrata is* essentially an active one. It is not the attitude of prostrating oneself before the gods and begging some favour of them. It is rather the attitude of fulfilling the desire through certain definite action. In fact, the concept of the other world or heaven is alien to the *Vrata*-s. Of course, some of the *Vrata*-s, as we find them today, are but religious hotchpotch. But, as Abanindranath has insisted, these are either cunning devices of recent origin or just contaminations with later ideas. In any case, these are not genuine *Vrata*-s. The really genuine ones, as he poetically says, are attuned to the music of the earth.

One element of the *Vrata* is that it must be done collectively, by a number of people participating with the same desire. The desire of an individual and the actions designed to fulfil it cannot constitute a *Vrata*. It becomes a *Vrata* only when a number of persons cooperate to produce the same effect.

It may be possible for an individual to perform a dance but not a drama. Similarly, it may be possible for an individual to pray and propitiate: but not to perform a *Vrata*. Both prayer and *Vrata* are designed to fulfil the desires. However, the first is confined to the individual and it culminates in begging for the desire to be fulfilled; the latter is essentially collective and it ends in actually fulfilling the desire.

The peasants of Bengal perform the *vasudhārā vrata*. It is during the mid-summer drought, when, as the *vrata*- rhymes describe it 'the Ganga is sunken and the sky but a heap of ashes.' Naturally, the *vrata* is designed to fulfil the desire for rain, for plenty of water. The peasants sing. They sing of the shower and in the song they see the scorched earth submerged and the children swimming merrily. And they also act. They create the rain. They hang a jar on the tree, fill it with water and bore holes in it. The jar is the cloud. Water drips from it. It rains. That is how they enact, in fantasy, the fulfilment of the desired reality.

4. Magic Transplanted in Class Society

All this is picturesque indeed—the process of collective labour accompanied by some kind of primordial complex of song and dance and painting. In my next lecture I shall try to show how the requirement of human progress necessitated the negation of magic to make room for organised religion qualitatively different from magic, though without totally obliterating all hangover of magic—specially its negative aspect as having been essentially an illusion. In any case, the ideology *par excellence* of the primitive pre-class society is magic, which being unaware of goddesses and gods, prayers and propitiation, cannot but be looked back as pre-religious after all.

At the same time, specially for understanding Indian culture, we must not forget another point. Howsoever picturesque magic may appear in its original context of collective labour, there remains the possibility of its being transplanted in the later sharply class-divided society: when it is thus transplanted, it assumes the most monstrous and malignant form, serving the only purpose of ensuring financial gain for a negligible minority of a totally parasitical class. In Indian history, this actually happened in the comparatively later Vedic period—or, to be more specific, from the period of *Yajurveda*—when there developed the cult of what is called *yajña*.

There developed no doubt an extensive literature not only proclaiming which desire is sure to be fulfilled by the performance of which *yajña*, but also giving meticulous details of the way of performing each *yajña*, along with the spells appropriate for each. The literature that eventually grew about *yajña* acquired a fabulous bulk and looks most awesome. But if we raise the simple question, 'what exactly is *yajña*?', there is only one answer to it. It is in essence, nothing but primitive magic, because the main claim on which it is based is that the performance of certain acts automatically—i.e. by the intrinsic efficacy of its own—leads to the fulfilment of the results desired. There is no scope whatsoever in this entire process of the intervention of any divine agency granting the fulfilment of the desire. There is no question, in other words, of any prayer, propitiation or divine grace. As a matter of fact, the priest-class which alone is supposed to know the intricacies of performing *yajña*, eventually developed a powerful philosophical school, one of the main points of which is to deny the very existence of God and even to explain away the substantial reality of the famous Vedic deities like Indra, Varuṇa, Mitra and so on.

All this has proved somewhat puzzling to some of the modern scholars. Why should the most orthodox of all Indian thinkers—i.e. those who represent the Vedic "priests" ordinarily called—be at all so enthusiastic about total atheism? The answer seems to be that though we are accustomed to call them "priests", they are as a matter of fact not so, i.e. in so far as by "priests", we are inclined to understand those who are aware of the mode of prayer, propitiation, etc. for pleasing God or the gods and goddesses. On the contrary, what thy really are, are transplanters of primitive magic to the new socio-economic conditions, i.e. conditions of sharpy class-divided society, wanting to make their living by attracting financiers of *yajña,* i.e. ritual acts pure and simple, with the promise that nothing more than the performance of this is required for the fulfilment of all sorts of desires. To create conviction in these financiers, magical rituals had indeed to be adorned with a lot of mumbo jumbo—awesome as well as trivial. Thus we read in this ritual literature a detailed procedure of performing the *yajña,* of all sorts of implements required for their performance, etc. To these are added weary and wild speculations, absurd analogies, legends and etymologies, often also mock-disputations over useless trivialities. All this makes the discussions on the *yajña*-s the most unreadable and the most cumbrous specimens of Indian literary products. However, when all these concoctions added are sealed off, we are left with magic pure and simple. But it is not magic in its original context, namely the collective labour of the primitive people which, though illusory, somehow proves to be an aid to the actual productive technique. Magic transplanted to the sharply class-divided society becomes nothing more than mere economic drainage, financially beneficial only to a class of social parasites, professing or pretending to have the mysterious knowledge required for the performance of *yajña* and demanding of course fat fees from the financiers credulous enough to believe that the mere performance of it ensures the fulfilment of all sorts of desires.

In my subsequent lectures, I shall have the opportunity to discuss all this in more detail. For the present, it is perhaps enough to emphasise only one point. The evidence of magic shows that there was a stage of human development when there was no religion. Religion, as we shall see in the next lecture, is the characteristic product of class-society. Even when transplanted in the class-society, magic—now assuming the name of *yajña*—represents not merely a pre-religious attitude but also an attitude positively hostile to religion, inasmuch as it denies God and divine grace in every possible form.

Summing up

We have started with the proposition that every religion is the product of the institution of the spirit of God in man. We have observed that this is historically true at least as far as the major organised religions of the world are concerned. We have argued, however, that though true it is not the whole truth, for to this is to be added the further fact that religion itself—like the class society for which it is a historical necessity—is a transitory phenomenon after all, coming into being with the emergence of class society and destined to wither away with the transition to the classless society of the future. The first point required to be established for this view is that there was a time when there had been no religion and this was the period of the primitive pre-class society. We have tried to show that during this period there was "magic" instead of "religion"; the difference between the two is palpably qualitative.

In my next lecture I shall try to discuss the question of the making of religion, or more concretely that of the historical necessity of the beginnings of religion with the beginning of class society. For this purpose I shall follow mainly the researches of Gordon Childe.

REFERENCES

1. *Tanjur* mDo cxxxii.9. See Th. Stcherbatsky PS 1-16.
2. cf. *Iśvara-bhaṅga-kārikā* by *Śubhagupta. Tanjur* mDo cxii.11.
3. K. Marx CCHPR. Extract in Marx and Engels OR 42.
4. G. Thomson ER 7-8.
5. L.H. Morgan 561-62.
6. G. Thomson SAGS i.84.
7. V. Gordon Childe WHH 70.
8. L.H. Morgan 561.
9. G. Thomson ER 9.
10. J. Harrison 94.
11. G. Thomson ER 9.
12. G. Thomson SAGS i. 440.
13. J. Harrison 36-7.
14. G. Thomson SAGS i.66.
15. For summary of the book in English, See D. Chattopadhyaya L 113 ff.

2

The Making of Religion

1. Preliminary Remarks: Gordon Childe

For a descriptive account of the making of religion, we have to move about five thousand years back—sometime roughly to the third millennium B.C. when this gradually took full shape. This means that we have primarily to depend for the purpose mainly on the archaeologists, who, by examining the material remains of the extinct societies—though often correlating these also with ethnographical and ancient literary evidences where available—try to reconstruct an account of such hoary antiquity, inclusive of what Gordon Childe aptly calls "the spiritual equipment" of man. By this he means not only the ideas "translated into tools and weapons that work successfully in controlling and transforming external nature" but also "what is often termed society's ideology—its superstitions, religious beliefs, loyalties and artistic ideals."[1]

But there are archaeologists and archaeologists, with all sorts of theories and counter-theories—conjectures and counter-conjectures—which often give us the impression of a jungle as it were. Out of this jungle, however, came out a giant whose name was V. Gordon Childe. In the present lecture designed to discuss the making of religion, we propose to follow him, with full awareness of there being a host of his critics, inclusive of just mediocrity parading with nothing more than high-sounding jargons.

But let us first try to be clear about one point.

Marx died in 1883 and his lifelong collaborator Engels in

1895. Archaeology as a science was then hardly in its infancy. In spite of the decipherment of Egyptian writing by Champollion in 1822 and Schlieman's investigation of the origin of Greek civilisation at Troy and Mycenae in the 1870s, the excavations undertaken during the latter half of the nineteenth century, principally at Nineveh, Nirmud, Nippur and Lagash, are rightly described as " an undignified scramble for archaeological loot". The systematic method of excavation was really developed by Petrie, whose *Methods and Aims in Archaeology* was published in 1904, about ten years after Breasted—to whom we owe the concept of "the Fertile crescent"—began teaching Egyptology at the University of Chicago (1894), though whose first significant work *Ancient Records of Egypt* was first published in 1906. The first significant work on Sumerian excavation was that of the Royal Tombs at Ur by Leonard Wooley in 1926, while in 1924 John Marshall, depending on the work of Daya Ram Sahni at Harappa and R.D. Banerjee at Mohenjo-daro, announced the discovery of the ancient Indus Valley Civilisation.

We have mentioned some of the important landmarks in the making of modern archaeology or of archaeology as a science in its real sense—only to emphasise one point. It did not take shape during the lifetime of Marx and Engels.

It is therefore of considerable interest to note that though the makers of Marxism did not have the advantage of drawing on archaeology in formulating their view of social evolution, archaeology itself—in the works of no less a person than Gordon Childe—had to come to Marxism, so that the global survey of the earlier period of social evolution could become sufficiently meaningful.

In the book *Method and Theory of V. Gordon Childe,* Barbara McNairn has given us a brief sketch of how Gordon Childe's interest gradually shifted from the primarily philological—archaeological studies (the first edition of *The Dawn of European Civilisation,* 1925; *The Aryans,* 1926) to that of the understanding of the technique or the mode of obtaining the means of subsistence as determining the social relations as well as the ideological and other superstructural elements like science and religion. Though fascinating, we have neither the scope nor the need of reiterating the account of it here. What is of immediate relevance for our own discussion is his point of departure from his earlier interest to the basically socio-economic approach, because that gives us the first authentic account of the making of religion from the essentially archaeological viewpoint. This shift in Childe's interest took place in the mid-thirties of the last century. As Barbara McNairn rightly observes, "It was not till 1936 in *Man Makes Himself*, that Childe gave the first full account of his new economic ideas, and hence he emphasised his debt to Marxism."[2]

This book *Man Makes Himself* is a very brief one and, though stuffed throughout with cold archaeological data, was written in an amazingly simple style. Childe evidently intended it for a wide reading public. One reason for this was the scare then created by the rise of fascism, which threatened Europe with another impending "Dark Age", while Childe wanted people not to give up the hope for the future or in human progress. At the same time, Childe was too conscientious an archaeologist not to speak of progress in general terms; he substantiated it on the strength of the most relevant archaeological evidences on a global scale. The turn to Marxism, however, appears to have added a new dimension to his understanding of the very concept of progress. In other words, instead of viewing progress as a unilinear move forward of humanity, he viewed it from the dialectical standpoint, or, in Marxist terminology, progress that carried on its heels just its opposite. As we shall presently see, Childe himself used the phrase "dialectics of progress" while explaining how, for the most momentous march forward of humanity, it was also a historical necessity to create religious views and superstitions which, in their turn, had also an inhibitory effect on further progress, though as the Marxists add, despite this inhibitory influence, human progress did continue, ultimately creating material conditions that can finally overthrow the need for these. But let us not anticipate here our entire discussion but remain confined to the archaeological analysis of Gordon Childe for the making of religion as a historical necessity for the move forward to civilisation.

In the third year of the Second World War, Childe wrote another book primarily for popular consumption, or, in his own words, "designed for the bookshop public", tracing in it human progress from the hunting-gathering stage to the end of the Roman Empire. The book bears the title *What Happened in History* (1942). Though by far the most outstanding survey of global archaeology upto the time of its composition (magnificently combining in it archaeology with relevant ethnographical data), its "popular" form was motivated by the same anxiety to allay the apprehension of another Dark Age or, in other words, to protect the concept of "progress". As he himself observed, "I wrote it to convince myself that a Dark Age was not a bottomless cleft in which all traditions of culture were finally engulfed ...So I wrote it with more passion and consequently, more pretentions to literary style than in my other works."[3]

All this has to be accepted as true, specially when it is authenticated by Childe's own words. At the same time, it is difficult to imagine that an archaeologist of his stature would have turned to Marxism simply because he was scared by the rise of fascism. As we are inclined to understand, Childe accepted Marxism not merely because it helped him to retain confidence in human progress but also because he found in it the best model for synthesising the vast archaeological data in the most meaningful manner.

I have specially mentioned these two books, because these are for me the best specimens of the archaeologists' account of human progress, understood, as already said, from the Marxist viewpoint—an account in which the historical necessity of the making of religion is most lucidly explained. One of the key points for understanding this is what Childe calls "the Urban Revolution". Etymologically, *Urban* is derived from *urbs* or city and the word Revolution is modelled on what is called "the Industrial Revolution" in Europe, though ethnologically "Childe did in fact quite often associate his urban revolution with Morgan's stage 'civilisation'"[4]. Thus, in short, it means the momentous socio-economic transformation as a result of which man first moves forward from the neolithic villages to the earliest cities, which, as he showed, took place in the Old World in three primary centres—Egypt, Mesopotamia and India, the last in the Indus basin. In his view, all later forms of urbanisation are but linear descendants of these three primary centres. The point that interests us most for our present discussion, however, is that in Childe's archaeological analysis the making of religion is not only a concomitant of this profound socio-economic transformation but also an essential precondition of it. We shall try to sum up his analysis, elucidating it where necessary.

2. The Urban Revolution

In 1936, Childe formulated this concept in his *Man Makes Himself;* in 1942 he elaborated it in *What Happened in History,* and, perhaps for the purpose of giving us some idea of its crucial importance for his archaeological understanding, contributed an article exclusively on it in 1950 in the journal *Town Planning Review* with the title "The Urban Revolution". In 1958, again, in his *Retrospect* (published in the *Antiquary,* xxxii, 69-74) he returned to it in the context of explaining the need he felt for rewriting his earlier work *The Most Ancient East: The Oriental Prelude to European Prehistory* (1928) in the form of *New Light on the Most Ancient East: The Oriental Prelude to European Prehistory* (1934).

What, then, is the Urban Revolution and how is it connected with the making of religion?

In the book *What Happened in History,* Childe begins with an account of the differentiation of man from the rest of the animal kingdom with making of the tools, which, as compared to the purely physiological organs of the animals, are called "extracorporeal organs that he makes, uses, and discards at will".[5] But the earliest tools, made of a broken bough or a chipped stone, are too rudimentary or too crude to enable man to gather food from nature, which could at best be enough to maintain the human communities at the lowest level in spite of the best efforts on their part. So men, though leaving the stage of animal existence, were originally nothing more than hungry naked food-gathering savages. However, man moved forward in improving his tools, though of course slowly—almost imperceptibly slowly—for many many thousand years, till the quantitative accumulation of such protracted changes in technique led him to reach a new qualitative stage, with new tools efficient enough to *produce* food instead of just *gathering* it. This was a very significant move forward—significant enough to be called "revolutionary", inasmuch as man no longer remained a mere savage, and reached the stage of neolithic barbarism. In Childe's words: "The escape from the impasse of savagery was an economic and scientific revolution that made the participants active partners with nature instead of parasites on nature."[6] From this stage onwards, the pace of human progress gained new momentum, eventually attaining what Childe called the stage of "the Higher Barbarism of the Copper Age." As he put it: "The worst contradictions in the neolithic economy were transcended when farmers were persuaded or compelled to wring from the soil a surplus above their own domestic requirements, and when this surplus was made available to support new economic classes not directly engaged in producing their own food. The possibility of producing the requisite surplus was inherent in the very nature of the neolithic economy. Its realisation, however, required additions to the stock of applied science at the disposal of all barbarians, as well as a modification in social economic relations. The thousand years or so immediately preceding 3000 B.C. were perhaps more fertile in fruitful inventions and discoveries than any period in human history before the sixteenth century A.D. Its achievements made possible that economic reorganisation of society that I term the urban revolution."[7]

Elsewhere, Childe gives us a more detailed account of human achievements on the eve of the urban revolution: "The neolithic revolution, just described, was the climax of a long process. It has to be presented as a single event because archaeology can only recognise the result; the several steps leading up thereto are beyond the range of direct observation. A second revolution transformed some tiny villages of self-sufficing farmers into populous cities, nourished by secondary industries and foreign trade, and regularly organised as States. Some of the episodes which ushered in this transformation can be discerned, if dimly, by prehistory. The scene of the drama lies in the belt of semi-arid countries between the Nile and the Ganges. Here epoch-making inventions seem to have followed one another with breathless speed, when we recall the slow pace of progress in the millennia before the first revolution or even in the four millennia between the second and the Industrial Revolution of modern times.

"Between 6000 and 3000 B.C. man has learnt to harness the force of oxen and of winds, he invents the plough, the wheeled cart, and the sailing boat, he discovers the chemical processes involved in smelting copper ores and the physical properties of metals, and he begins to work out an accurate solar calendar. He has thereby equipped himself for urban life, and prepares the way for civilisation which shall require writing, processes of reckoning, and standards of measurement—instruments of a new way of transmitting knowledge and of exact sciences. In no period of history till the days of Galileo was progress in knowledge so rapid or far-reaching discoveries so frequent."[8]

3. Neolithic Revolution and "Surplus"

What was it in the neolithic revolution that ultimately made such spectacular achievements possible? The crucial point for understanding it is that the neolithic revolution "enabled human labour to produce more than was necessary for its maintenance", or, in short, what is called "surplus". It was this surplus that relieved some members of the community from being direct producers of their own means of subsistence, which could henceforth be met from the pool of the surplus produced by the rest of the community. Those who were thus freed from the need of directly producing their means of subsistence could become *whole-time* specialists in various capacities and contribute to the general fund of the spectacular achievements, leading man in certain centres to the threshold of the urban revolution.

For our present purpose, which is to understand the making of religion, it is not necessary to go into the details of the technological developments that led man to the eve of civilisation. However, two points are in need of special clarification. The full-time specialists had to be attracted to the incipient urban centres and had to be made permanent settlers there. For this purpose they had to be provided with some new mode of "protection" than before. Secondly, the social surplus produced in the villages had to be channelised to the incipient city centres and stored there, so that the means of subsistence for the whole-time specialists could be supplied from this accumulated surplus. The smoothest or by far the most convenient way for meeting both the purposes was to resort to some ideological device, and, under the given historical conditions, the most suitable ideological device then conceivable was a body of religious beliefs and practices. The preconditions for the making of this was at least partially already present in primitive magic, or, to be more specific, in its purely negative aspect, i.e. in so far as it was sheer illusion. In other words, primitive magic was itself infected with an inner contradiction. On the one hand, though an illusory technique it could and did serve as a supplement to real technique in the collective context. However, as rooted out of the collective context, it was shorn of its original economic function, though its essential illusoriness acquired a new socio-economic function, serving as the ideological device of providing with some new model of "protection" to the resident whole-time specialists made to settle in the incipient urban centres as well as for channelising the social surplus of the villagers to these centres for the maintenance of them as whole-time specialists. Incidentally, this new socio-economic function of religion as an outgrowth of magic is not to be misunderstood: it was a historical necessity for the urban revolution which was a tremendous progress for humanity—though progress not in a unilinear sense but in the dialectical sense of carrying on its heels marks of pronounced retardation.

Gordon Childe in his essay *The Urban Revolution* discussed at length the first of the two preconditions of this profound socio-economic transformation, namely "protection" in the new form without which the whole-time specialists could not be made to settle in the incipient urban centres. In his other books, specially in *Man Makes Himself* and *What Happened in History* he discussed the dialectics of progress as exemplified by the making of religion.

4. "Protection" for Full-Time Specialists

Let us first take up the question of the "protection" in new form of the resident whole-time specialists in the urban centre, borrowing freely for the purpose the expression used by Childe.

In any Stone Age Society, paleolithic or neolithic, "every member of the local community, not disqualified by age, must contribute actively to the communal food supply by personally collecting, hunting, fishing, gardening or herding. As long as this holds good, there can be no full-time specialists", for there is no surplus to feed them. "On the contrary, community of employment, the common absorption in obtaining food by similar devices guarantees a certain solidarity to the group. For cooperation is essential to secure food and shelter and for defence against foes, human and sub-human. This identity of economic interests and pursuits is echoed and magnified by identity of language, custom and belief; rigid conformity is enforced as effectively as industry in the common quest for food. But conformity and industrious cooperation need no State organisation to maintain them. The local group usually consists either of a single clan (persons who believe themselves descended from a common ancestor or who have earned a mystical claim to such descent by ceremonial adoption) or a group of clans related by habitual intermarriage.

"Now among some advanced barbarians (for instance, tattooers or wood carvers among the Maori) still technologically neolithic, we find expert craftsmen tending towards the status of full-time professionals, but only at the cost of breaking away from the local community. If no single village can produce a surplus large enough to feed a full-time specialist all the year round, each should produce enough to keep him a week or so. By going round from village to village an expert might thus live entirely from his craft. Such itinerants will lose their membership of the sedentary kinship group. They may in the end form an analogous organisation of their own—a craft clan, which if it remains hereditary, may become a caste, or, if it recruits its members mainly by adoption (apprenticeship throughout Antiquity and the Middle Ages was just temporary adoption), may turn into a guild. But such specialists, by emancipation from kinship ties, have also forfeited the protection of the kinship organisation which alone under barbarism, guaranteed to its members security of person and property. Society must be reorganised to accommodate and protect them."[9]

Thus the development of the city centres required that such specialists had to be rescued from nomadism with a guarantee of security in a new social organisation, because they had to break away from the old kinship bond and therefore also from the older mode of protection offered by the collective life. Security in this new form was provided by the state—a form of organisation totally unknown to humanity before the urban revolution, and, judged from the three primary centres of the earliest cities unearthed in the Old World—Egypt, Mesopotamia and Indus—the earliest states must have been theocratic, i.e. in theory controlled by some goddess or god though in practice by their earthly representatives—the priest, priestly corporations or sometimes the god-king. Thus the full-time craftsmen, uprooted from the older tribal collectives which provided them with the protection they required, came under the substitute protection of the state, which in its turn, required for its inner cohesion, a new ideological device: awe-inspiring organised religion. In the state organisation, the major share of the social surplus collected naturally went to the rulers—the priests or their corporations—while the actual workers were provided with barely nothing more than the means of subsistence, but the tension between the two was effectively submerged by the same ideological device, namely the making of religion. We quote Gordon Childe at some length:

"So in the city, specialist craftsmen were both provided with raw materials needed for the employment of their skill and also guaranteed security in a State organisation based now on residence rather than kinship. Itinerancy was no longer obligatory. The city was a community to which a craftsman could belong politically as well as economically.

"Yet in return for security they became dependent on temple or court and were relegated to the lower classes. The peasant masses gained even less material advantages; in Egypt, for instance, metal did not replace the old stone and wood tools for agricultural work. Yet, however imperfectly, even the earliest urban communities must have been held together by a sort of solidarity missing from any neolithic village. Peasants, craftsmen, priests and rulers form a community, not only by reason of identity of language and belief, but also because each performs mutually complementary functions, needed for the well-being (as redefined under civilisation) of the whole. In fact, the earliest cities illustrate a first approximation to an organic solidarity based on a functional complementarity and interdependence between all its members such as subsist between the constituent cells of an organism. Of course, this was only a very distant approximation. However necessary the concentration of the surplus really were with the existing forces of production, there seemed a glaring conflict on economic interests between the tiny ruling class, who annexed the bulk of the social surplus, and the vast majority who were left with a bare subsistence and effectively excluded from the spiritual benefits of civilisation. So solidarity had still to be maintained by the ideological devices appropriate to the mechanical solidarity of barbarism as expressed in the preeminence of the temple or the sepulchral shrine, and now supplemented by the force of the new State organisation. There could be no room for sceptics or sectaries in the oldest cities."[10]

We now pass on to the second—and perhaps more important—point necessitating the making of religion as a precondition for the urban revolution. It is concerning the channelisation of the social surplus from the rural producers to the growing cities.

5. Channelisation of the Social Surplus

There were three conceivable alternative techniques that could make this possible: 1) direct plunder, 2) purchase and 3) persuasion by ideological devices. We are going to see why the third of these presumably best suited the city governors and that moreover we have the clue in this to the making of religion.

Let us begin with the three possible alternatives for procurement.

The possibility of purchase of the surplus products of the direct producers by the city governors—the priests perhaps having merchants or traders under their control—is ruled out, because the proposition of purchase would presuppose accumulation of sufficient wealth (or in the ancient context, the accumulation of city-products with which to barter with the peasants), and this, in its turn, already employing full-time specialists by the merchants and traders to produce the typical urban products or commodities with which to buy or barter with the peasants, or, in other words, the accumulation of food stuff in the city granaries already accomplished.

We are thus left with the other two alternatives, namely plunder and persuasion.

Of these two, again, plunder is a cumbrous and complicated process: it presupposes the maintenance of a bureaucracy with at least a sizeably large armed force to coerce the peasants to part with their surplus products; for their maintenance we have to presuppose again sufficient food stuff already accumulated in the city granaries.

At any rate, compared to it, the method of persuasion is infinitely simpler and smoother. All that this method requires is the effective use of superstition. Thus, for example, once the peasants are made to believe that without offering a part of their products to the goddesses or gods—i.e. concretely to their earthly representatives, the priests or priestly corporations working for the god or god-king—they remain exposed to grave perils like droughts, plagues and disasters in many other forms, the peasants would willingly—and perhaps also eagerly—part with whatever they can afford from their own products. Besides, these priests or priestly corporations do not have to create such superstitions out of nothing: from the paleolithic age people with extremely rudimentary understanding and control of nature were trying to supplement their real technique with the illusory technique, namely magic, from the purely negative aspect of which goddesses, gods and all sorts of supernatural agencies could smoothly take shape. As George Thomson very lucidly explained: "The technique of magic is developed by the ruling class as a means of consolidating their privileges by investing them with supernatural sanctions. In this way the working class, being ignorant of the true causes of its subjection, is reconciled to its lot. This is the genesis of religion. Religion is an outgrowth of magic which emerges with the class struggle.

It is an inverted image of social reality. Just as magic expresses primitive man's weakness in the face of nature, so religion expresses civilised man's weakness in the face of society."[11] This must have made the task of the governors of the early nucleus of cities all the more easy. They had only to systematise—to add awe and wonder—to a pre-existing system of beliefs and practices, and thus make the technique of persuading the direct producers to part with their surplus products to city rulers from which to maintain the full-time specialists essential for the Urban Revolution.

I may perhaps be allowed here to mention a personal experience. While visiting the Tirupati temple a few years ago, I had the opportunity of looking at the devotees forming a queue—perhaps a mile long, if not longer—each patiently waiting for his turn to offer to the god either in cash or in kind something which in our terminology could be ultimately nothing but the surplus of their own labour. There was absolutely no question of any purchase or of barter. There was no question of using the police or any other coercive machinery enforcing them to part with their earnings—in short, there was nothing at all but their devotion to the deity that made them eager and anxious to part with their "surplus". Obedience to the god and offering to him assumed the status of a privilege. How absurdly simple the whole process was of accumulating wealth in the temple treasury, which ran to millions. While looking at the queue, I had myself the feeling that something like this—though perhaps not in the same grand scale—must have happened in front of the monumental structures unearthed by the archaeologists, which are relics of the temples of the earliest cities in Egypt, Mesopotamia and presumably also in the Indus basin. Strong religious beliefs effectively propagated among the masses must have been the easiest or the least cumbersome technique of getting the social surplus from the rural areas channelised to the growing cities.

The dramatic change in the nature of the archaeological materials testifies to the newly emerged organised religion:

"The most striking objects now unearthed are no longer the tools of agriculture and the chase and other products of domestic industry, but temple furniture, weapons, wheel-made pots, jewellery, and other manufactures turned out on a large scale by skilled artisans. As monuments we have, instead of huts and farmhouses, monumental tombs, temples, palaces, and workshops. And in them we find all manner of exotic substances, not as rarities, but regularly imported and used in everyday life. Evidently the change in the archaeologists' material reflects a transformation in the economy that produced the material."[12]

At the same time—i.e. notwithstanding the waste and inequities—it needs to be remembered that all this had been a historical necessity. Without the newly developed imposing religions the channelisation of wealth to the city centres could not be possible; without this channelisation there could be no provision for whole-time resident specialists in these centres, and without the whole-time resident specialists the foundation of civilisation could hardly be laid. Whatever, therefore, might have been the eventual role of religion, it would only be wrong sociology to overlook or ignore its original historical necessity.

7. The Dialectics of Progress

"It is important to remember", observes George Thomson, "as Gordon Childe has pointed out, that even the lowest paid slaves in Mesopotamia were better off than the free and equal members of any neolithic village. The urban revolution had brought about an absolute rise in the standard of living. On the other hand, if we take into account the enormous rise in the productivity of labour, it is clear that relatively they were worse off. The gains won from the revolution were unequally distributed. It was this factor that eventually brought the expansion of the new economy to a stop."[13]

Gordon Childe gives us an inventory of human achievements preceding and following the urban revolution. Before the urban revolution comparatively poor and illiterate communities had made an impressive series of contributions to man's progress. The two millennia immediately preceding 3000 B.C. had witnessed discoveries of far-reaching consequences," of which Childe mentions fifteen—beginning with artificial irrigation and ending with what belonged to "the earliest stages of the revolution"—a solar calendar, writing, numeral notations' and bronze.[14]

"The two thousand years after the revolution, say from 2600 to 600 B.C., produced few contributions of anything like comparable importance to human progress. Perhaps only four achievements deserve to be put in the same category as the fifteen just enumerated." These are: 'decimal notation' of Babylonia, an economical method for smelting iron on an industrial scale, a truly alphabetic script and aqueducts for supplying water to cities.[15]

Thus contrasting progress before and after the urban revolution, we have to admit that the latter "seems to mark, not the dawn of a new era of accelerated advance, but culmination and arrest of an earlier period of growth". Why, then, was this arrest? Curiously enough, one of the most important causes accounting for this is to be found in the same factor that caused the revolution.

The revolution was caused not merely by the human capacity to produce surplus but also by the channelisation of this surplus to the centres that grew into cities and the accumulation of it under the custody of the gods, i.e. their earthly representatives, the priests and the priestly corporations. But how did it happen like that and what were its consequences? This leads us to Gordon Childe's brilliant summing up of the "dialectics of progress", which we have to read and re-read for our own understanding of the subsequent course of ideological development.

"Almost from the outset of his career, it would seem, man used his distinctively human faculties not only to make substantial tools for use upon the real world, but also to imagine supernatural forces that he could employ upon it. He was, that is, simultaneously trying to understand, and so use, natural processes and peopling the real world with imaginary beings, conceived in his own image, that he hoped to coerce or cajole. He was building up science and superstition side by side.

"The superstitions man devised and the fictitious entities he imagined were presumably necessary to make him feel at home in his environment and to make life bearable. Nevertheless the pursuit of the vain hopes and illusory short-cuts suggested by magic and religion repeatedly deterred man from the harder road to the control of nature by understanding. Magic seemed easier than science, just as torture is less trouble than the collection of evidence.

"Magic and religion constituted the scaffolding needed to support the rising structure of social organisation and of science. Unhappily the scaffolding repeatedly cramped the execution of the design and impeded the progress of the permanent building. It even served to support a sham facade behind which the substantial structure was threatened with decay. The urban revolution, made possible by science, was exploited by superstition. The principal beneficiaries from the achievements of farmers and artisans were priests and kings. Magic rather than science was thereby enthroned and invested with the authority of temporal power.

"It is as futile to deplore the superstitions of the past as it is to complain of the unsightly scaffolding essential to the erection of a lovely building. It is childish to ask why man did not progress straight from the squalor of a 'pre-class' society to the glories of a classless paradise, nowhere fully realised as yet. Perhaps the conflicts and contradictions, above revealed, themselves constitute the dialectics of progress. In any case, they are facts of history. If we dislike them, that does not mean that progress is a delusion, but merely that we have understood neither the facts nor progress nor man. Man made the superstitions and the institutions of oppression as much as he made the sciences and the instruments of production. In both alike he was expressing himself, finding himself, making himself."[16]

8. The Pharaoh That Failed

We shall end the present lecture with a few words on the historical necessity of organised religion for the human move forward to civilisation. We have already quoted Childe's observation that in the earliest centres of the urban revolution there can be no room for sceptics or sectaries. The reason for this is also explained by him. The ideological cohesion essential for the urban revolution was affected by organised religion, which, if disturbed in any way cannot be tolerated. But what happens to one who chooses to disturb this universe of organised religion either by questioning it or by trying to replace it by some new cult, even though he has the profoundest political and financial power under his command? The answer is that his proposed reform was destined to fail and this for the simple reason that it was historically premature or that he was trying to go against history. In other words, material conditions were not yet created for the acceptance of such reform.

We are indebted to Barrows Dunham for a brilliant analysis of a case of this with which he opens his work *Heroes and Heretics*. It is the case of a pharaoh that failed. We shall follow Dunham and quote him freely for discussing this example, because all this has far-reaching implications for our understanding of the future of religion—a subject to which we propose to return in our last lecture.

By the rarest of chances—though for reasons we can at best speculate—an Egyptian king proposed to introduce some basic reform in the then prevailing organised religion of Egypt. When we look back at it today, his proposed reform may not appear to be so momentous after all. But it was not really a trifling one judged in its historical context.

The basic facts are as follows: "The king was Amenhotep IV, a pharaoh of the eighteenth dynasty, about 1372 to 1354 B.C. This name he changed, in celebration of his heresy, to Akhnaton. That is to say, he preferred being called 'Aten is well pleased' to being called 'Amon is satisfied'. The reason was that the pharaoh, having a taste for physical explanations, conceived the ruling god as a sun-disc rather than as a spirit of the sun."[17]

Being an all-powerful king after all, he had not much problem in introducing this reform. He had only to decree it. But its consequences were disastrous. As Dunham describes: "The main facts are reasonably clear. Akhnaton outlawed the old theology, closed down the temples of the traditional gods, abolished the priesthoods, services, and profits connected with them. He built in the plain of Amarna a new shrine and capital, Akhetaten, the City of the Horizon of the Sun. Priestly wrath and consternation can hardly have been less than they would be if some modern government were to abolish, all at once and all together, Catholicism, Protestantism, Judaism, and every other religion hitherto existing. Yet the priests, thus stricken had no alternative and no redress. The pharaoh's will was paramount."[18] Thus in short, Akhnaton's proposed reform amounted to an abrupt abolition of ancient rites and old theogonies, deprived the priests of their older functions and therefore also their financial interests inherited from their previous reigns. The ideological cohesion on which the urban revolution in Egypt was based was seriously disturbed, the old temples deserted. At the same time, the pharaoh's decree was absolute. There was no scope whatsoever to question or flout it—not at least so long as the pharaoh was there. Deprived of their inherited power and privileges, they were angry of course, but they were also obliged to keep this anger suppressed or subdued.

With the pharaoh's passing away, this anger burst forth with great vengeance. They erased Akhnaton's name from the calendar of kings, allowing it to appear—when at all—as "that criminal of Amarna". "The City of the Sun's Horizon was razed to the foundation, which still lingers at Amarna and the succeeding pharaoh, Tutankaten, changed his name to the celebrated Tutankhamon we now know. Thus the god Aten, the divine sun-disc, lost to the god Amon, the spirit of the sun."[19]

Such then is in broad outline the history of the innovation sought to be introduced into the official religion of Ancient Egypt, or to what may appear to us as some kind of a comparatively mild tilt to naturalism given to this official religion. The anger or vengeance of the priests provoked by this proposed innovation is, of course, easily understood: it was directly connected with their material interest—the income they derived from being the custodians of the traditional religion and performance of the older rites. However, the question that interests us most in this connection is the reaction of the people—of the vast masses of direct producers—whose surplus product was channelised to the temples and fattened the priests. Any relative relief from religious superstitions which kept them cowed to the priests—however feeble it may appear to us—is expected to be some relief for them after all. But it seems that historically speaking this did not happen and the pharaoh failed mainly because the people were not with him or that he could not mobilise the masses in favour of his proposed reform. At their stage of historical development they needed religion because of the material conditions in which they lived. And the religion they were accustomed to had deep roots in their consciousness, any sudden change in which was only to cause alarm in them and hence could not be acceptable. As Barrows Dunham observes:

"What were people to think and do when the gods they had worshipped, sworn by, lived by, were all at once declared nullities? One's child was perhaps ill, and one had always appealed to Amon on such occasions. One's husband had died, and it had always been necessary to settle such accounts with Osiris. But now, by decree of Akhnaton, Amon and Osiris were nowhere to be found. Their priests were scattered, their temples wasted grass. In the old days, Amon had healed and Osiris saved. Could one be sure that Aten would do these things?

"The people felt, one imagines, left naked to circumstance. A trusted guard had been removed, and the new seemed no protection because untried. Thus men kept a secret faith in the old religion and the old rites; they were on the priests', side whatever the pharaoh might decree. And in the end, when Akhnaton had died, priests and people did to his works what he had done to some of theirs."[20]

We have now a fuller idea of the failure of the pharaoh. Religion cannot be changed—far less uprooted—by sheer decree, so long as the material conditions of the society remain unaltered. That is why Marx called it the heart of a heartless world or a necessary palliative—the opium—required by the people in such a world. It can be uprooted only by changing the material conditions that require religion. Though today we may be nearing such material conditions, the ancient Egyptians were very far from it. Religion was a necessity for them, though not for us today. But more of the future of religion later.

REFERENCES

1. V. Gordon Childe WHH 15.
2. B. McNairn 29.
3. Quoted *ibid* 33.
4. *Ibid* 92.
5. V. Gordon Childe WHH 8.
6. *Ibid* 48.
7. *Ibid* 68.
8. V. Gordon Childe MMH 105.
9. V. Gordon Childe ACI 14.
10. *Ibid* 17.
11. G. Thomson ER 9.
12. V. Gordon Childe MMH 142.
13. G. Thomson SAGS i. 24.
14. V. Gordon Childe MMH 227.
15. *Ibid.*
16. *Ibid* 236-37.
17. B. Dunham 3.
18. *Ibid* 4.
19. *Ibid* 5.
20. *Ibid* 4-5.

3

Harappan Religion and the Aryan Question

1. Preliminary Remarks

The excavations and explorations by the archaeologist, both in India and Pakistan, during the decades after the first discovery of the Indus Valley Civilisation (often also called the Harappan Civilisation or Harappan Culture, taking Harappa as its type-site), have added more to our knowledge of it, than was contained in the three volumes edited by Marshall *(Mohenjodaro and the Indus Valley Civilization)*, the first full-length study of it based on the collaboration of a number of specialists like Mackay, Guha, Hempy and others. So has also grown a flourishing literature on the subject—literature sometimes based not merely on the analysis of cold archaeological data but also on presumptions and conjectures, inclusive unfortunately also of some apparently wild ones. In a recently published book called the *Ancient Cities of the Indus* edited by G.L. Possehl (1979), we have a *Bibliography* of the literature on the Indus valley civilisation, which contains 1607 entries. From this we have a rough idea of the dust cloud raised by scholars specially when it comes to such questions as the social organisation, ideology, decadence and final destruction of the civilisation as also on its language and script. In such circumstances it is only empty optimism to expect anybody to discuss the religion of the Harappan culture without being immediately challenged by a whole host of critics, however far they may be from agreeing with each other. Thus, for example, Marshall wrote a long chapter on the religion of the ancient Indus Civilisation the main thrust of which is that many prominent elements of what is known as later Hinduism—like the prominence of the Great Mother Goddess, the worship of Śiva sometimes conceived as Paśupati (the lord of animals) and sometimes as the mere phallic emblem, zoomorphism in varied forms, etc.—though forming prominent features of Hinduism are not at all traceable in the Vedic literature, conceived earlier as the main source of the Hindu religion. Only after the excavations of the Harappan sites have we been able to realise that these have real roots in the ancient Harappan Civilisation and somehow survived to form the later religious beliefs and practices of the Indians. Among the contemporary archaeologists the Allchins think that, though written decades ago, this essay of Marshall continues to be a "brilliant" one.[1] Childe himself summed up Marshall's essay with his own comments thus:

> Religion gives the most convincing illustration of the explicitly Indian character of the Indus Civilisation. Many objects from the ancient cities, otherwise unintelligible, can be satisfactorily explained by reference to the Hindu cult. The innumerable clay figurines, indeed, are not without parallels elsewhere. In India the majority represent a female personage, often richly bejewelled and sometimes pregnant or nursing an infant; some may be votive statuettes of deities, but others may represent petitioners, or even dolls. So, too, among clay models of animals the frequent Brahmani bulls may be regarded as sacred but others, such as oxen provided with a moveable head, are obviously toys like the equally common miniature carts, couches, loaves, and vases. But there are aniconic objects, notably huge stone phalli and rings, often wavy along the edge, that correspond to the *liṅgas* and *yonis* of Hindu fertility cults.
>
> The 'seals' and tablets of stamped clay, engraved copper or moulded fayence offer more conclusive evidence. A 'seal' from Mohenjo-daro depicts a horned deity with three faces sitting

> cross-legged in the attitude of ritual meditation between various wild animals; he is obviously the prototype of Siva, 'three-faced', lord of beasts, 'prince of yogis', as Marshall has demonstrated in detail. Several clay tablets depict a male deity; one shows a river gushing out of a goddess's womb. In other cases tree spirits are clearly indicated. In contrast to such themes, all familiar to Hindu iconography, are isolated motives suggestive of Babylonia—an antithetic group of 'a hero tempting tigers and a half-human monster like the Sumerian Enkidu grappling with a bull or a tiger. The swastika and the cross, common on stamps and plaques, were religious or magical symbols as in Babylonia and Elam in the earliest prehistoric period, but preserve that character also in modern India as elsewhere.
>
> The religious concepts suggested by the foregoing documents are familiar to modern and post-Vedic Hinduism. But they are conspicuously absent from the oldest of the Hindu sacred books, the *Rig-Veda,* while scenes illustrative of its hymns may be sought in vain in the Indus period. Śiva as depicted at Harappa and Mohenjo-daro is generally regarded as an 'aboriginal' deity taken over by the invading Vedic Aryans and verbally identified with the unimportant Vedic Prajāpati. Tree-spirits and female deities played a negligible role in Vedic mythology, and phallicism is unmentioned—all have been regarded by European scholars as post-Vedic accretions in Brahmanism.
>
> Conversely, the celestial figures of the Vedic pantheon, like the thunder-wielding Indra, are not detectable in the Indus period. The horse, so prominent in Vedic imagery and a principal sacrificial animal, is never represented on the 'seals' which yet must have had a religious virtue.
>
> For the above reasons alone the Indus Civilisation may be regarded as non-Aryan and pre-Aryan. In fact, it provides a documentary illustration of the sources, long inferred on comparative grounds, of those 'accretions' which distinguish modern Brahmanism from the religion and ritual illustrated in the Vedas.[2]

As against all this, A. Ghosh has come out rather sharply. As he says:

It is useless to reiterate and scrutinise all that has been said to substantiate that many later-day Hindu religio-ritualistic practices and spiritual thoughts were derived from the Harappa. The worship of Śiva-paśupati, the liṅga and the mother-goddess, Upaniṣadic speculations, asceticism, Jainism, Tantrism, Sāṃkhya, Yoga—quite a motley of thoughts, beliefs and practices—all have been thought to be Harappan in origin. These theories are all fanciful and do not bear scrutiny. For example, Rudra has the appellation *Paśupati* in later Vedic literature not in the sense of lord of beasts in general but of cattle only, which is the primary sense of *paśu*, though a comprehensive meaning of birds and domestic and wild animals is not unknown. Nor has the Vedic Rudra anything to do with meditation. Thus, to see Śiva-paśupati in the well-known and much-spoken-of seal of Mohenjo-daro, which depicts wild animials, is unjustified. Similarly, Sankalia has shown that the so-called *liṅga*-s of Mohenjo-daro were found in streets and drains and were not enshrined in rooms, as one would expect sacred objects to be.[3]

2. The Harappan Civilisation

When archaeologists—inclusive of very eminent ones—argue among themselves so sharply, prudence demands that we better avoid at the present stage of our discussion the question concerning the *nature of* Harappan religion and of its possible survival in later Hinduism. What we nevertheless propose to argue first of all is that religion must have been a very potent factor in the administrative infrastructure of the Harappan Civilisation. It may be useful for this purpose to begin with a brief idea of the extent and population of this civilisation itself.

In 1883, depending mainly on published reports, the Allchins observe: "The area enclosed by line joining the outermost sites at which the material culture of this civilisation has been discovered is little less than half a million square miles, considerably larger than modern Pakistan."[4] Within this vast area of about 500,000 square miles, Pande and Ramachandran, in 1971, claimed that there were 258 sites as distinctly Harappan though, in 1979, D.K. Chakrabarti said, "While some sites..... should now be added to the list there is no assurance that all these 258 sites should strictly come under the category of the Harappan."[5] In 1992, M.R. Mughal observed: "The evidence shows that the area covered by the Indus Civilisation was larger than any of the known civilisations of the ancient world...This enormous area could not have been limited to only 144 sites (the number so far securely identified) and, indeed, claims have been made for the discovery of twenty-seven sites of Harappan affinity in east Punjab and the Doab near Saharanpur."[6]

It may be premature for us to expect a gazetteer of this vast region. But it is necessary to note a few points about the sites in it so far located.

First, D.K. Chakrabarti, depending on the published reports, has prepared a list of the major sites, i.e. those covering roughly over 1,25,000 square feet, along with the estimated population of each. The population-estimate is based on "a nineteenth century statistics for Srikapur in northwest Sind" which Lamrick thought "closely resembled Mohenjo-daro both in dimensions and layout." According to this estimate the total population of Mohenjo-daro could be 35,000 though according to Datta it could be 34,469 and according to Fairservis it was likely to have been 41,250. The total area covered by Mohenjo-daro was 850,000 square metres. Assuming Lamrick's estimate of the density of population of Harappan settlements, one is thus led to think that a site of 1,25,000 square feet was likely to have 5000 or more people in each. On the basis of this, Chakrabarti has observed, "One can possibly say with some emphasis that there were at least 15 Harappan settlements with more than 5000 people each. The number is likely to have been more when full data are available for most of the sites."[7]

Secondly, Fairservis has attempted to sketch the composition of the non-agricultural population of Mohenjo-daro. According to him this comprised of 1) Priests, 2) Scribes and Seal-cutters, 3) Musicians and dancers, 4) Engineers,

5) Potters, 6) Weavers, 7) Brick-makers, 8) Masons, 9) Carpenters, 10) Metallurgists and 11) Traders. To this needs to be added the amazing uniformity observed throughout all Harappan sites: "the apparent uniformity of weights and measures, the common script, the uniformity—almost common currency—of the seals, the evidence of extensive trade in almost every class of commodity throughout the whole Harappan culture zone, the common elements in architecture and town-planning, the common elements in art and religion."[8] It may not be wrong to expect the same uniformity in the population-composition pointed out by Fairservis about Mohenjo-daro in the other Indus cities.

Thirdly, admitting the same or at least very similar population-composition in major Harappan sites, it needs to be noted that none of the eleven major groups in the city mentioned was expected to be the direct producer of its own means of subsistence. In all presumption, therefore, they were likely to have lived on the food produced by the villagers within the general cultural zone—i.e. on the social surplus funnelled to the city centres.

This brings us back to the question we have previously discussed, namely that of the channelisation to the city-centres of the social surplus produced by the villagers. We have argued that there could be three conceivable modes for the machinery of this channelisation: purchase, plunder and persuasion—i.e. persuasion on the strength of religious beliefs. Of these three modes, as we have already argued, only the last was likely to have been the most feasible and least cumbrous one. Applying the same argument to the Harappan culture zone, we are left to presume that religion was likely to have been the most potent force in the administrative machinery of the vast "Harappan empire", whatever might have been the actual nature of this religion, i.e. whether its nature answered to Marshall's description of it or not.

3. Kosambi and Needham

Of the three primary centres of the urban revolution, there is now not much doubt that administrative machinery of at least two—namely Egypt and Mesopotamia—was largely under the grip of the priests or priestly corporation. But our present problem is concerning the third primary centre, namely the Indus Valley Civilisation.

By analogy, one is tempted to argue that since it was necessary for the other two primary centres of the Urban Revolution to use massive superstition for policing the state, the same must have been true also of the third primary centre. Besides, as we have already seen, the accumulation of the surplus products of the direct producers in the cities, seems to be best explained by the presumption of the use of superstition.

Nevertheless, the assumption of the vast Indus "Empire" being ruled by the priests or priestly corporations could not be a smooth one and there is literally a storm of controversy over the question of the actual socio-political organisation of Harappan culture. The main difficulty here, as about many other questions concerning the Harappan Culture, is the want of direct literary documents attesting to some view or the other. It is generally admitted no doubt that there must have been some strong centralised power enforcing its authority over the Harappan "empire", because, without assuming it there is hardly any explanation of the manifold uniformity observed throughout it. But we have no direct knowledge of the nature of this centralised authority.

Many relics of the Indus civilisation are generally viewed no doubt as indicative of religion and religious beliefs.

From the time of the publication of the first full report on the excavations of Harappa and Mohenjo-daro to that of the recent excavations at Kalibangan and Lothal, the archaeologists have shown how a large number of the relics of this forgotten civilisation cannot but be understood as pointers to the powerful religious beliefs prevalent in the period. We need not present here a list of such relics; readers interested in these may look up the recent book by the Allchins,[9] where all these are very ably summed up. This does not mean, of course, that we have now a coherent and comprehensive understanding of the nature of Harappan religion and it is no use speculating on when and how any full account of it would be reconstructed. Nor is the basic fact to be ignored that among the eminent archaeologists controversies are still going on about its general outlines. However, all these do not materially affect our main argument which requires only to be admitted that the Indus relics are unmistakably indicative of some presumably strong and widespread religious beliefs. If so, we have also to admit that the custodians of these were the priests or priestly corporations, and, on the analogy of ancient Egypt and Mesopotamia, we are naturally tempted to assume that these priests and priestly corporations could remain quite aloof from the actual administration of the vast Indus "empire". On the contrary it would be logical to think that, whatever might have been the actual nature of the social structure of the Indus civilisation, these priests or priestly corporations were only likely to have a large share—if not the decisive one—in the administrative machinery in the Harappan administration. From the remains of the imposing houses of the merchants in the Harappan cities, it is sometimes conjectured that these merchants could have formed the actual ruling class of the "empire". But the obvious difficulty about such a conjecture is that it can hardly explain the eventual internal decadence of the Harappan civilisation, about which the archaeologists are agreed. The merchant class—sensing as it does greater and still greater profitability—are drawn to improving and augmenting the production-process and hence the government under their rule is only expected to prosper rather than become a prey to eventual degeneration and decay. By contrast, a government under the priestly class is only likely to be under the grip of strong conservatism and hence also exposed to the possibility of creeping paralysis, because innovations in technique are generally frowned upon by the stereotyped religious beliefs.

Incidentally, D.D. Kosambi has advanced a new suggestion indicative of the effective use of religious superstition as an instrument for Harappan administration. As he observes,

> Finally, the tools of violence were curiously weak, though nothing is directly known of their social mechanism for wielding force, which we call the state. The weapons found in the Indus cities are flimsy, particularly the ribless leaf-blade copper spearheads which would have crumpled up at the first good thrust. There is nothing like a sword in the main Indus strata. Archers occur in the ideograms, arrowheads of stone and copper have been discovered. The bow would be a survival of the hunting age. Of course, iron was not known, so that a few weapons in the hands of a small minority might have sufficed; but the contrast with the excellent, sturdy though archaic, tools proves that the use of weapons was not very important. Therefore, the state mechanism, whatever it was must have had some powerful adjunct that reduced the need for violence to a minimum. The cities rested upon trade, not fighting; but if the army of police were not very strong what helped the trader maintain his unequal sharing of profit?
>
> The answer seems to lie in religion. Though there are no great statues of the gods, what has been called the 'citadel' mound undoubtedly corresponds to the temple-*zikkurat* structures in Mesopotamia... The Harappan site has been devastated by brick-robbing, while at Mohenjodaro, what must have been the ruins of a major building in the sacred enclosure are covered by a *Kuṣāna stūpa.* But the adjacent 'Great Bath' at Mohenjodaro (filled with water drawn laboriously by hand from a special adjacent well, beautifully constructed with bitumen waterproofing between brick layers, a drain for emptying, and surrounded on three sides by cells) must have been a ritual tank, because of the beautiful and well-used bathrooms in every private house which distinguish the city from anything in the proto-history of Mesopotamia, or Egypt. Even a bather from the citadel could easily have descended the steps in the wall which led down to the river. I have explained this as the

> prototype of the sacred lotus pond *puṣkara* which survived in the later times.[10]

Thus one of the main points stressed by Kosambi in favour of his view of the comparatively greater need of religious superstitions for policing the Harappan "empire" is the flimsiness of the offensive weapons specially as contrasted with the excellent sturdy though archaic tools, which proves that the weapons usually needed to keep the people under control were not very important after all.

To this may be added another point.

The weapons unearthed at the Harappan sites are indeed flimsy, indicating the lesser use of direct violence and hence of comparatively greater use of religious superstitions. What could have perhaps made the argument stronger is another consideration.

Already in the introduction to the first full-length report on *Mohenjo-daro and the Indus Civilisation*, Marshall observes: "Their weapons of war and of the chase are the bow and arrow, spear, axe, dagger and mace. The sword they have not yet evolved; *nor is there any evidence of defensive body armours*."[11] We have added emphasis on the last point, because, thanks to Needham's brilliant analysis, this seems to have very decisive importance for the point Kosambi has argued in favour of the relatively greater use of religious superstitions for the Harappan rulers. The offensive weapons mentioned by Marshall—spear, axe, dagger and mace—are useful in hand-to-hand fights, or in cases of immediate confrontation of armed forces with the exploited peasants when necessary. Besides, these were flimsy after all. But not so are the bow and arrow, which are very effective long distance missiles. Now, as Kosambi admits, the bow and arrow being inherited from the hunting stage, there is nothing to prevent the assumption that the peasants were as much equipped with these as were the armed forces of the ruling class. And it is here the *defensive body armour* has supreme importance from the viewpoint of military technology in the distant past. So long, therefore, as the defensive body armour is not developed and used, some method other than direct violence is needed to keep the masses under control.

In the Chinese context, as Needham shows, the lack of inadequate development of defensive body armours was one main reason for the ruling ideology—viz. Confucianism—to preach to the people to remain submissive to the lords. As he observes,

"What was the situation, then in ancient China? There the crossbow—a most powerful weapon—was invented centuries before anywhere else. We know that the men of the feudal levies in ancient China (by that I mean between 800 and 300 B.C.) were armed with powerful bows. But at the same time protective armour was very little developed. The archaeologist Laufer has written a fine monograph on Chinese armour. It arises very late, and in early times you only get protective clothing made of bamboo and wood. Moreover, there are in the *Tso Chuan* countless stories of feudal lords being killed by arrow shots. *If the mass of the people as a whole were in possession of a powerful offensive weapon, and the ruling class were not in possession of a superior defensive means, one can see that the balance of power in society was different from what it was in, e.g. the time of the early Roman Empire, where the disciplined legions were rather well armoured, with bronze and iron. A slave population was possible because it was not in possession of the arms and armour of the legionaries,* nor did it have access to powerful bows. The principal Roman weapons were always the spear and the short sword. We know what troubles the slaves could give on the few occasions in which they did gain access to substantial stores of weapons, as in the revolt of Spartacus. In China, it was a different story, because from an early date the people had crossbows and the lords had poor defensive armour. If that was the case, it means that the people in China had to be persuaded, rather than cowed by force of arms, and hence the importance for the Confucians."[12] For, as Needham has already shown, "during what may be called the high feudal period in China, which runs roughly from the eighth century to the third century B.C. the feudal lords were assisted and counselled by a group of men who afterwards became the school of philosophers which we know as the Confucian School."[13] It preached to the people the virtue of remaining as pious law-abiding citizens.

With these points in mind, we may now return to the question of the Indus civilisation.

Not that we know of there having been any philosopher in the Harappan culture, not to speak of any school of philosophy even remotely resembling the Confucian one. Notwithstanding Marshall's expectation to the contrary, it can perhaps be safely asserted that there was nothing like that, or at least, even if there was any philosopher in the Harappan culture, we shall never know anything about him. What we do know, however, is that the *Harappans did not develop any defensive body armour*. Even imagining that they developed something like that made of flimsy materials, these could not be effective against the long-distance missiles—the arrows—possessed in common by the army and the masses. It follows, therefore, that for keeping the masses under control it was essential for the ruling class to have something more than their military technology. This something more had to have the efficacy of persuading the masses to remain as pious law-abiding citizens. In other words, in default of effective defensive armour they had to depend on ideological devices—or, to put it more bluntly, on religious superstitions on a really massive scale. Many stray objects found in the Harappan regions give us some glimpse of a rather imposing religion, though our archaeologists are yet to reconstruct any agreed view of this religion. But religion was there and so also there must have been its main accessory, namely, superstition.

Could it, then, be that this religious ideology was the main instrument in Harappan culture for the purpose of policing the state notwithstanding the controversies among the archaeologists and others concerning the actual *nature of* this religion ? This brings us back to Kosambi's hypothesis though from a different premise altogether. What Kosambi argued from the flimsiness of offensive weapons seems to be strengthened by the lack of defensive body armour.

4. End of Harappa and the Aryan Question

That after a glorious career of over five hundred years, the Indus civilisation came under the grip of decline and degeneration is archaeologically indisputable. Depending mainly on Mackay's work, Gordon Childe gives us some typical examples of this: "The last reconstructions of Harappan cities exhibit every sign of decadence. Old bricks were re-used for building mean houses on the sites formerly occupied by the spacious mansions of the bourgeoisie. The civic authority could no longer enforce the building regulations so strictly observed in more prosperous days so that the dwellings encroached upon the streets."[14] Discussing the fate of Mohenjo-daro city, Wheeler observes: " One thing at least is clear about the end of Mohenjo-daro: the city was already slowly dying before its ultimate end. Houses, mounting gradually upon the ruins of their predecessors or on artificial platforms in the endeavour to out-top the floods, were increasingly shoddy in construction, increasingly carved up into warrens for a swarming lower-grade population. Flimsy partitions subdivided the courtyards of houses. To a height of 30 feet or more, the tall podium of the Great Granary on the western side of the citadel was engulfed by rising structure of poorer and poorer quality. Re-used brickbats tended to replace new bricks. The city, to judge from excavated areas, was 'becoming a slum'."[15]

Why then was this decadence and degeneration after a splendid career of five hundred years or more? This is a question about which there is a good deal of controversy among the contemporary archaeologists. Perhaps it is premature at the present stage of research to expect any clear and definite answer to it. What is possible nevertheless is to mention some of the prominent views advanced with comments on their comparative plausibility.

To begin with, let us note that what was perhaps true of the Mohenjo-daro city was not likely to be true of the entire vast area covered by Harappan culture. Nevertheless, we cannot possibly ignore the fate of the Mohenjo-daro city itself. At least one of the factors that contributed to the decline of this city was repeated flooding of it which, as the Allchins observe, "has been long known and cannot be entirely discounted as a cause of local destruction."[16] It is true that the Harappans could and did rebuild or repair the city repeatedly after the devastating floods; but that must have sapped much of their energy and vitality, and hence also caused deviation from their main preoccupations. It is also tempting to conjecture that this could have further considerably weakened—or at least adversely affected—the prestige of the city rulers if they were priests, priestly corporations or priest-kings, because one source from which they were likely to create a belief in their supernormal power in the popular mind could have been their capacity for predicting the coming of the floods based on their astronomical knowledge and calendrical science. If, in spite of this, they failed to predict the coming of floods—not to mention preventing these with their allegedly supernatural power—the city dwellers were likely to have raised awkward questions about their authority.

So, the ravages caused by floods were likely to have been one of the factors that brought degeneration to the Mohenjo-daro city itself. But some of the archaeologists appear to go a step further and want to view the floods—along with other climatic and tectonic changes—as having been basically responsible for the degeneration and destruction of the Harappan culture as such. It is not necessary for our present purpose to attempt a re-examination of their view, because one of our most competent archaeologist-scientists, D.P. Agrawal,[17] has already done it.

We have in his discussion some knowledge of the changes in physical geography affecting the fate of the Indus civilisation At the same time, it needs to be noted that the decline and fall of the Indus civilisation must have been a complex phenomenon and to seek its full explanation only in any of these—or exclusively in one type of causal factors—remains exposed to the danger of over-simplification. As Agrawal himself says, "It may, however, be emphasised that not a single cause but several contributed towards the decline and disappearance of the mighty Harappan civilisation."[18] This is a point on which a significant number of serious archaeologists concur. "Just as the creation and maintenance of the system was the outcome of the successful combination of several factors," observe the Allchins, "so too its breakdown could have been caused by the weakening of any one of these or the upsetting of their harmonious balance and interaction."[19] Even Wheeler—about one of whose points, as we shall presently see, there is a great deal of furore among our historians—substantially agrees with this.

> Let it be said at once that the factors instrumental in the dissolution of historic civilisations have never been of an uncomplicated kind. It can scarcely be supposed therefore that prehistoric or historic civilisations have endured simple destinies; in other words, here too no single explanation can convincingly claim total truth. Over-ambitious wars, barbarian invasions, dynastic or capitalistic intrigue, climate, the malarial mosquito have been urged severally in one context or another as the overall cause. Other theories have relied upon racial degeneration, variously defined or cautiously vague; an enlargement, perhaps, of Samuel Butler's plaint that 'life is one long process of getting tired'. Recently, deep floods derived from violent geomorphological changes have been blamed for the end of the Indus civilisation. In a particular context which has sometimes been amplified or decried without warrant, I once light-heartedly blamed Indra and his invading Aryans for a concluding share in this phenomenon. The list need not be extended. It is safe to affirm that any one of these answers to the problem is far more likely than not to be fallacious in isolation. The fall, like the rise, of a civilisation is a highly complex operation which can only be distorted and obscured by easy simplification.[20]

Interestingly enough among the causes of the decline and fall of the Indus "empire", Possehl mentions even the possibility of peasant revolt against the exploiters in the cities. As he says, "Political conflict which could destroy the people producing the food and/or the productive potential of the land on which the non-agricultural urbanites ultimately depended could be another such explanation. Might we not entertain such notions as peasant revolts against the ruling classes who may have been largely or even exclusively city based?"[21]

Such then, are some of the conjectures concerning the decline and end of the Indus civilisation, though also with the caution often expressed against putting an exclusive emphasis on any of these possible factors. The list of conjectures can indeed be enlarged, adding to such possibilities as the financial setback resulting from the loss of foreign trade from the time when the "Mesopotamians looked more towards Arabian and African markets than to Magan and Meluhha"—Meluhha probably having been "the generalised term for the Indus culture area." Another factor suggested is "the 'wearing out' of the land due to over-cultivation", though the Allchins observe that this " seems unlikely as the population pressure can never have been very great, and in late times the land retained great fertility."[22] At the same time, the Allchins comment, "Another possibility which cannot be ignored is of epidemic diseases following in the wake of floods."[23]

All these are conjectures, of course. Besides, it remains an open question whether these factors, taken severally or jointly, can explain only the internal decay of the civilisation or its final and full destruction. Gordon Childe thinks, "This imposing civilisation perished utterly as a result of internal decay accelerated by the shock of barbarian raids."[24] He mentions the following archaeological evidences for the last point:

> Then the civilisation was destroyed by barbarian invaders and the cities reoccupied by illiterate aliens. At Harappa these are

represented only by extended and flexed burials in Cemetery H and the queer painted vases that accompany them. At Chanhu-daro and Jhukar, in Sindh, a distinct barbarian culture, the Jhukar culture replaced the Harappa civilisation. Everywhere the literate tradition exemplified in the inscribed 'seal' was extinguished. But judging by the pottery from Cemetery H and Jhukar sites and by metalwork from the latter, some technical traditions were carried over. Presumably potters and smiths survived to work for new customers. Naturally, they produced quite novel objects to suit foreign tastes.

The pottery from Jhukar and Cemetery H is still wheel made, painted and fired in the old techniques, but shaped quite differently and adorned with new designs. Jhukar smiths made shaft-hole axe-heads and probably axe-adzes and pins with swollen necks. Button or bead seals of stone, fayence or pottery replaced the rectangular glazed steatite 'seal' and were engraved with geometric designs, including the filled cross, or rarely with conventional beasts, inscriptions and lifelike animals.

The button seal like the shaft-hole axe is plainly a north-western intruder in India. The closest parallels to the Jhukar seals, and an exact parallel to the axe-adze, comes from Hissar III in northern Iran. Putative intermediate links will be cited later from Makran and Baluchistan.

These agreements suggest that the barbarians who destroyed the Harappa civilisation included at least invaders from north-western Iran. Wheeler has boldly suggested their identification with the Vedic Aryans. In any case, the *ṛṣis* sang their Vedic hymns in a prehistoric night; for the invasion completely broke the literary tradition, and there is no fixed point in Indian history till the reign of Darius.[25]

5. Aryans and the End of the Indus Civilisation

The view expressed by Wheeler and tacitly endorsed by Childe, namely that the decaying or already largely decayed Indus civilisation came to its final end by the invasion of the Indo-Aryan speaking people—or more simply by the Vedic peoples—has provoked a great deal of controversy and even much indignation among a section of our scholars.

Wheeler fist expressed this view rather forcefully in 1947 in *Ancient India* No. 3 though in 1968 (reprinted in 1979), confronted with some strong criticisms and perhaps also taking note of other possible factors pointed out by other archaeologists as contributing to the final destruction of the Indus valley civilisation, he gave the impression of withdrawing or somehow modifying his original emphasis and observed that he had once blamed Indra rather rhetorically. The tone appears to be somewhat subdued and we shall try to see whether that is at all necessary. But let us begin by quoting his view as originally expressed. In 1947 he observed:

> The Aryan invasion of the Land of the Seven Rivers, the Punjab and it environs, constantly assumes the form of an onslaught upon the walled cities of the aborigines. For these cities the term used in the *Ṛgveda* is *pur*, meaning a "rampart", "fort" or "Stronghold". One is called "broad" *(pṛthvī)* and "wide" *(urvī)*. Sometimes strongholds are referred to metaphorically as "of metal" *(āyasī)*. Autumnal *(śāradī)* forts are also named: "this may refer to the forts in that season being occupied against Aryan attacks or against inundations caused by overflowing rivers". Forts "with a hundred walls" *(śatabhujī)* are mentioned. The citadel may be made of stone *(aśmamayī)*: alternatively, the use of mud-bricks is perhaps alluded to by the epithet *āma* ("raw", "unbaked".) Indra, the Aryan war-god to *puramdara.* "fort-destroyer". He shatters, "ninety forts" for his Aryan protege, Divodāsa. The same forts are doubtless referred to where in other hymns he demolishes variously ninety-nine and a hundred "ancient castles" of the aboriginal leader Śambara. In brief, he "rends forts as age consumes a garment."
>
> Where are—or were—these citadels? It has in the past been supposed that they were mythical, or were "merely places or refuge against attack, ramparts of hardened earth with palisades and a ditch." The recent excavation of Harappa may be thought to have changed the picture. Here we have a highly evolved civilisation of essentially non-Aryan type, now known

> to have employed massive fortifications, and known also to have dominated the river system of north- western India at a time not distant from the likely period of the earlier Aryan invasions of that region. What destroyed this firmly-settled civilisation? Climatic, economic, political deterioration may have weakened it, but its ultimate extinction is more likely to have been completed by deliberate and large-scale destruction. It may be no more chance that at a late period of Mohenjo-daro men, women and children appear to have been massacred there (Mackay 1938: 94f., 116 ff. 172). On circumstantial evidence, Indra stands accused.[26]

The evidence cited by Mackay of men, women and children having been massacred at a later period of Mohenjo-daro is perhaps not so important for the central argument for viewing the Harappan cities finally ransacked by the invading Aryans. As P.V. Kane and others have shown, the presence of the scattered skeletons at Mohenjo-daro can be explained by other hypotheses. Nevertheless the question of the Aryan invasion remains and it is as strongly supported by some archaeologists as it is bitterly contested by some others. We shall first mention some of the latter.

In 1964, G.F. Dales wrote an article with the title "The Mythical Massacre at Mohenjo-daro."[27] Free use of innuendo and other rhetorics apart, the writer frequently refers to the authority of Marshall and Hargreaves, evidently ignoring the fact that some of their observations have become dated. However, from the archaeological viewpoint, his main—or at least one of his main—arguments is: ".... What is the material evidence to substantiate the supposed invasion and massacre? Where are the burnt fortresses, the arrowheads, weapons, pieces of armour, the smashed chariots and bodies of the invaders and defenders? Despite the extensive excavation at the largest Harappan sites there is not a single bit of evidence that can be brought forth as unconditional proof of an armed conquest and destruction on the supposed scale of the Aryan invasion." Depending mainly on his own theory of floods etc., Dales concludes: "The enemy of the

Harappans was Nature... —Indra and the barbarian hordes are exonerated."[28]

As if it were not enough to establish the innocence of Indra, K.M. Srivastava, depending mainly on the theories of natural calamities to explain the end of the Indus civilisation, proclaims: "Indra, therefore, stands completely exonerated."[29] However he wants to go a step further and seek the clue to the genesis of Wheeler's theory of the Aryan invasion. As he puts it:

> In retrospect, when we look at Wheeler's career as an archaeologist in England and India and we see him as a Brigadier in the British army during World War II, we feel he could not interpret the dubious evidence of Mohenjo-daro and Harappa in any other manner. He started his real archaeological career from Maiden Castle excavations and soon emerged as an authority of Roman archaeology. His *Rome Beyond the Imperial Frontiers* clearly shows how deeply involved he was in the Roman art and architecture, Roman concepts of town-planning—citadels, lower towns, assembly-halls, etc. Thus when he was confronted with the twin-mound towns of the Harappans and the huge fortification walls and mud-brick platforms as well as the photographs of the so-called 'massacre' at Mohenjo-daro he was at once reminded of Roman history and archaeology. Marshall's (1931) and Vats's (1940) reports on Mohenjo-daro and Harappa, respectively, as well as Piggott's *Prehistoric India* (1950: 244: 248) provided him sufficient speculations on Aryan warfare and Indra's attack on Harappan towns. The common textbooks on Indian history adorned his personal library. For the former army man and the Director General of Archaeology in India, as Wheeler was, the Aryan invasion of Indus towns (1961: 249) was as simple as the Roman invasion of Britain and Turkey.[30]

A. Brigadier in the British army almost obsessed with the Roman model is naturally not expected to know much of the Vedas. Wherefrom, then, did he get the Vedic materials to substantiate his theory of the Aryan invasion? Srivastava has a simple answer to this: "In fact it was V.S. Agarwal who provided these references to Dr. Wheeler when the latter requested Professor Agarwal, then an officer in the Archaeological Survey of India, on tour at Harappa, although Dr. Wheeler never acknowledged it in any of his writings."[31]

All this is evidently imputing a certain lack of honesty to Wheeler. Our point, however, is that if Wheeler is really to be criticised for not acknowledging the real source of his information about the Vedic materials (as he unfortunately did), we are to look elsewhere. The theory of the Aryan invasion of the Indus Valley Civilisation—and this based upon a considerable amount of Vedic data—(inclusive of those used by Wheeler)—was already advanced by R.P. Chanda in 1926 and 1929. Since these were published as *Memoirs of the Archaeological Survey of India*, Nos. 31 and 41, Wheeler's want of acquaintance with these is not easily conceivable.

The fact that within a few years of the discovery of the Indus Valley Civilisation the sound Vedic scholarship of R.P. Chanda led him to the view that the ruin of the cities was finally due to the attack of the Vedic people under the leadership of their war-god Indra, and this was, to say the least, a remarkable academic performance on his part. But most of the writers on Indian archaeology do not mention this and the hypothesis is generally associated with the names of Wheeler and Piggott, who more or less plagiarised R.P. Chanda. Therefore we propose to reproduce here the writing of R.P. Chanda at some length.

6. R.P. Chanda and the Theory of the Aryan Invasion

Here are some of the observations of R. P. Chanda published in 1926 in No. 31 of the *Memoirs of the Archaeological Survey of India* (pp. 1-5):

> The archaeological discoveries at Harappa in the Punjab and at Mohenjo-daro in Sind have pushed back the monumental history of India from the third century B.C. to at least the beginning of the third millennium B.C. by one single stroke. A series of literary monuments, the Vedic Saṃhitas, the Brāhmaṇas, and the Sutras have long been known, the youngest

in age among which is probably older than the third century B.C. But a wide divergence of opinion relating to the age of these works and particularly of the *Ṛgveda* among scholars renders their use as sources of history unsafe....

To facilitate the coordination of the data of Archaeology with literary evidence I propose to discuss in this paper some of the passages in the Vedic literature that throw light on the early history of the Indus valley....."Many of the stanzas of the *Ṛgveda* contain references to Pura and Pur both of which terms mean *nagara*, 'town', in classical Sanskrit. In one stanza (7.15.4) an extensive *(śatabhujī)* Pur made of copper or iron *(ayas)* is referred to. In another stanza (1.58.8) prayer is offered to Agni to protect the worshipper with Purs of *ayas*. In such passages *ayas* is evidently used in a metaphorical sense to denote strength. Śuṣṇa, a demon, is said to have a moveable *(cariṣṇva)* Pura (8.1.28). In the *Ṛgveda* Pura is much oftener connected with the enemies of the Aryan than with the Arya Ṛṣis and warriors. Two of the famous Ṛigvedic kings, Divodāsa, the chief of the Bharatas, and Purukutsa, the chief of the Purus, are found engaged in war with hostile owners of Puras. Divodāsa was the son of Vādhryasva and grandfather of the more famous Sudās who defeated a confederacy of ten tribes including the Yadus, Turvasas and Purus on the Western bank of the Puruṣṇi (Ravi). It is said (4.30.20) that Indra overthrew a hundred Puras made of stone *(aśmanmayī)* for his worshipper Divodāsa.

The Puras that Indra overthrew for Divodāsa evidently belonged to Śambara who is called a Dāsa (non-Arya or demon) of the mountain (6.26.5). In one stanza (9.61.2), among the enemies of Divodāsa are mentioned the Yadu (the Chief of the Yadus) and Turvasa (the chief of the Turvasas) with Śambara. The greatest feat that Indra performed on behalf of Purukutsa, the chief of the Purus, is thus described in a stanza (6.20.10): 'May we, O Indra, gain new (wealth) through your favour; the Purus worship thee with this hymn and sacrifices. You destroyed the seven autumnal (*śāradī*) Puras with thunder weapon, slew Dāsas and gave wealth to Purukutsa.' The epithet *śāradī*, usually translated as 'autumnal', is explained by Sāyaṇa in different ways. In his commentary on the above stanza he explains the term *śāradī* as 'belonging to a demon named Śarat.' But in other places (1.131. 4 etc.) he explains it as 'annual Puras of the enemies strengthened for a year with ramparts, ditches, etc.' The authors of the *Vedic Index* are of the opinion that *Śāradī* or autumnal Puras 'may refer to the forts in that season being occupied against Arya attacks or against inundations caused by overflowing rivers'. The same exploit performed by Indra on behalf of the chief of the Purus is also referred to in certain other stanzas...

"The terms Pur and Pura mean *nagara*, 'city', 'town', and not fort. The Sanskrit equivalent of 'fort' is *durga* which also occurs in the *Ṛgveda* (5.34.7; 7.25.2). In one stanza (1.41.3) not noticed by the authors of the *Vedic Index*, Durga and Pura occur side by side. Sāyaṇa here takes Pura as an epithet of Durga meaning 'neighbouring'. But if we can shake off our bias relating to the absence of towns in the Rigvedic period we can recognise in this stanza references to both fort and town. The recovery of the ruins of cities at Harappa and Mohenjo-daro leaves no room for doubt that the Rigvedic Aryans were familiar with towns and cities of aliens. It is futile to seek any more historical elements in the legends of Divodāsa and Purukutsa than perhaps the names of these heroes. But if we eliminate the mythical and fanciful additions there is no reason to doubt the possibility of the nucleus. There existed, and the folk memory remembered that there once existed, Arya worshippers of Indra who waged wars against civilised aboriginal neighbours living in towns and fighting from within strongholds. Who, then, were these enemies of the Aryas? Do the hymns of the *Ṛgveda* give us any more information about them?

"It appears to me that the aboriginal towns-folk with whom the Aryas came into collision in the Indus Valley are called Paṇis in hymns of all the books of the *Ṛgveda*. Yāska (*Nirukta* 6.27) in his comment on *Ṛgveda* 8.66.10 says, 'The Paṇis are merchants', and in his comment on R.V. 10. 108.1 (*Nirukta* 11.25) he calls the Paṇis demons. The distinction between the human and the superhuman Paṇi is also recognised by Sāyaṇa, the author of the commentary on the *Ṛgveda* and the context justifies the distinction. The word Paṇi is evidently derived from *Paṇa*, 'Price.' The human Paṇis of the *Ṛgveda* are wealthy merchants who do not offer sacrifices and do not give gifts to priests. In RV. 1.124.10 the poet addressing Dawn says, 'Let the Paṇis who do not perform sacrifices and do not give gifts sleep unawakened (for ever)'. Another poet sings, 'Ye mighty ones (Aśvins) what do you do there; why do you stay there among people who are held in high esteem though not offering sacrifices; ignore them, destroy the life of the Paṇis' (RV. 1.83.3). A poet prays to Indra (1.33.3), 'Do not behave like Paṇi' *(mā Paṇiḥ bhūḥ)*, which according to the scholiast means, 'Do not demand the price of kine.' Another poet expecting a suitable reward for his offering of Soma drink, addresses the same deity as Paṇi (8.45.14). The Soma-drinker Indra does not like to make friends with the rich Paṇi who does not offer Soma sacrifice (4.28.7). A poet prays (3.58. 2), 'Destroy in us the mentality of the Paṇi' *(jarethām asmat vi Paṇeḥ manīṣām)*. Sometimes the Ṛṣis (Poet) betray a conciliatory mood. In one hymn (6.53) the god Puṣan is repeatedly requested 'to soften the heart of the Paṇi' and make the Paṇis obedient. This hymn occurs in a book (6) of the *Ṛgveda* composed by *Ṛsis* of the family of Bharadvāja. In one hymn of this book (6.45.31-33) the poet, a Bharadvāja, praises Bṛbu, a Paṇi chief, for giving thousands of liberal gifts. Indian tradition long remembered this acceptance of gifts by Bharadvāja from the Paṇi Bṛbu as an exceptional case, an example of the special rule that a Brahmin who has fallen into distress may accept gifts from despicable men without being tainted by sin. We are told in the code of Manu (10.107), 'Bharadvāja, a performer of great austerities, accepted many cows from the carpenter Bṛbu, when he was starving together with his sons in a lonely forest.' (Bühler). Sāyaṇa in his commentary on RV. 6.45.31 describes Bṛbu as the carpenter of the Paṇis.

"It is evident from the hymns of the *Ṛgveda* that the Aryas were divided into two main classes, the priests and the warriors. Cattle breeding appears to be the main source of their livelihood, cows being the chief wealth. Agriculture was practised to a limited extent. A hymn (9.112) refers to the different professions followed and the crafts practised by the Aryas. Trade finds no place in the list. So the conclusion that the much maligned Paṇis were the representatives of an earlier commercial civilisation seems irresistible. Among the antiquities unearthed at Mohenjo-daro are coins with pictographic legends that indicate the very early development of commercial life in the Indus Valley. The Paṇis probably represented this pre-historic civilisation of the Indus Valley in its last phase when it came into contact with the invading Arya civilisation. During the second millennium B.C. there occurred in the Indus Valley events analogous to those that occurred in the Aegean world at about the same time, that is to say, successive waves of invaders of Aryan speech poured from the north-west. These invaders who in the *Ṛgveda* call themselves Arya met in the southern part of the valley a civilised people who lived in cities and castles and mainly depended on commerce for their livelihood. The Arya conquerors who were inferior in material culture either destroyed the cities or allowed them to fall into ruin. Their great god Indra is called Purohā or Purandra, 'sacker of cities'. Like the pre-historic civilisation of the Aegean, the pre-historic civilisation of the Indus Valley also failed to survive the shock of the Aryan invasion."

7. Archaeology an Aid to Vedic Studies

Let us briefly focus on the point we have been trying to argue. The discovery of the Indus Valley Civilisation, besides dramatically extending our knowledge of ancient Indian history, has also another dimension. It has become a tool for us for the interpretation of Vedic literature—specially parts of the *Ṛgveda*. The Vedic scholars may profitably turn to the archaeological findings to see if these can provide us with any clue to certain otherwise unexplained—or at best fancifully explained—passages of the *Ṛgveda*. Thus, for example, the *Ṛgveda* speaks of a considerable number of cities in the Land of the Seven Seas and of the ransacking of these by the Aryans under the leadership of the war-god Indra. The whole thing cannot be brushed aside as a mere figment of imagination of the Vedic poets for the simple reason that those who have never seen any city cannot refer to these: the Vedic peoples themselves could by no stretch of imagination be city-dwellers, it being overwhelmingly obvious from the internal evidence of the *Ṛgveda* that they were pastoral nomads after all. Therefore, before the discovery of Mohenjo-daro and Harappa—soon followed by the discovery of many other cities within the Harappan cultural zone—there could at best be some speculations about these *pura*-s or cities and of Indra's role as *purandara* or the sacker of cities in the *Ṛgveda*—speculations, some specimens of which are to be found in the *Vedic Index* by Macdonell and Keith. With the discovery of ruined cities in the Harappan cultural zone by the archaeologists the Vedic scholars are relieved of the obligation of indulging in such speculation, notwithstanding the circumstance that many questions concerning the archaeological findings still remain controversial or perhaps not yet fully explained. Thus, for example, the real story that the scattered skeletons found in Mohenjo-daro may remain a problem for the archaeologists, so also that of the corpses of the Aryan soldiers and their arms still eluding the archaeologists' spade. We may hope that more digging and better inferences of the archaeologists would solve such problems. What in the meanwhile is gained by archaeology in the matter of throwing light on the *Ṛgveda* must not be ignored, for the Ṛgvedic references to the cities and of the ransacking of these seem to have no better explanation than is provided by the material remains in the Harappan cultural zone. To correlate archaeology with literary evidences is often considered to be a tricky and delicate matter. However, the importance of archaeology as a tool for interpreting or understanding certain Vedic passages remains yet to be more adequately examined. As a tool it sometimes proves to be of surprising importance. We shall mention here another example.

8. D.D. Kosambi and the Vṛtra Myth

Let us not forget, however, that the Vedic poets were poets after all. And as poets, they belonged to the ancient world. So they are not expected to understand and objectively describe all phenomena; they record these in their own way. We are thus bequeathed by them with the tricky task of disentangling reality from myth in their poetry. We shall mention here one example of how D.D. Kosambi attempts it.

Like Purandara or "ransacker of cities", Indra is often called in the *Ṛgveda* Vṛtrahan or "slayer of Vṛtra." For the Vedic poets, this was apparently one of his great achievements. As Macdonell shows, "the chief and specific epithet of Indra is *Vṛtrahan*, 'Vṛtra-slayer'. It is applied about 70 times to him in the *Ṛgveda*."[32] Vṛtra is usually taken as the name of a dragon, destroying whom often with the aid of other gods, specially of the hoard of semi-deities called the Maruts, was considered one of his major performances. But there are certain peculiarities about this performance which cannot be easily overlooked. Vṛtra literally means the Obstructor, and is also described as *ahi*, literally 'serpent'. In other words, it is an obstructor, which also looked like a huge serpent. Many things are said by the Vedic poets about this serpent-like obstructor, among which some are extremely interesting. Vṛtra, it is said, was complacent with the idea that its real vulnerable part was known to none; however, along with the Maruts, Indra discovered its vulnerable part (iii. 32.4; v. 32.5) and thus he struck and destroyed the 'obstructor' with such fierceness as to shake the heaven and world. And what was the result? The whole area was flooded with water which was being obstructed by the serpent-looking obstructor. Here is how Macdonell gives some of the passages referring to the great exploits of Indra: "He smote Vṛtra who encompassed the waters (vi. 20.2; etc.); or the dragon that lay around *(pariśayānam)* the waters (v. 19.2); he overcame the dragon lying on the waters (v. 30.6). He slew the dragon hidden in the waters and obstructing the waters and the sky (ii.11.5), and smote Vṛtra who enclosed the waters, like a tree with the bolt (ii.14.2). Thus 'conquering the waters' (*apsujit*) is his exclusive attribute.... For many dawns and autumns Indra has let loose the streams after slaying Vṛtra (iv. 19.8).... He cleaves the mountain, making the streams flow or taking the cows (i. 57.6; x. 89.7), even with the sound of his bolt (vi.27.1). When he laid open the great mountain, he let loose the torrents and slew the Dānava, he set free the pent up springs, the udder of the mountain. (5.32.1-2). He slew the Dānava, shattered the great mountain, broke open the well, set free the pent up waters (i. 57.6; v. 33.1). He released the streams which are like imprisoned cows (i. 61.10), or which, like lowing cows, flow to the ocean (i. 32.2). He won the cows and Soma and made the seven rivers flow (i. 32.12; ii.12.12). He released the imprisoned waters (i. 57.6; i. 103.2), released the streams pent up by the dragon (ii.11.2)... let the flood of waters flow in the sea (ii. 19.3), caused the waters pent up by Vṛtra to flow (iii.26.6;iv. 17.1)."[33] And so on. The entire section of Macdonell dealing with Indra's exploit of destroying Vṛtra—snake-looking obstructor—needs to be read in full to see that according to the Vedic poet the main result of this was the release of pent-up water.

Incidentally, Macdonell points to the use in the *Ṛgveda* of the word *arṇas* or flood in this connection.

Shorn of poetic imagination and the inevitable proclivity to myth-making in ancient poetry, what does all this really mean? D.D. Kosambi answers:

"Vedic Indra is described again and again as freeing the streams. This was taken as a nature- myth in the days of Max Müller, a poetic representation of the rain-god letting pent-up waters loose from imprisoning clouds. Recorded but ignored details of the feat make such an explanation quite impossible. Indra freed the rivers from the grip of a demon Vṛtra. The word has been analysed by two most competent philologists [with full knowledge of Iranian (Aryan) as well as Sanskrit records] who did not trouble to theorise about the means of production. Their conclusion from purely philological considerations was that *vṛtra* meant 'obstacle', barrage', or 'bloquage', not a demon. The actual Ṛgvedic description independently bears this out in full. The demon lay like a dark snake across the slopes. The rivers were brought to a standstill *(tastabhānāḥ)*; when the 'demon' was struck by Indra's shattering weapon *(vajra)*, the ground buckled, the stones rolled away like chariot wheels, the pent-up waters flowed over the demon's recumbent body (cf. R.V. 4.19.4-8; 2.15.3). This is a good description of dams (not embankments as Piggott would have it) being broken up, while such prehistoric dams, now called Gebr-band, are still to be found on many water- courses in the western parts of the region under consideration. The evidence for Indra's breaking up dams is not merely rationalisation of the Vṛtra myth. RV. 2.15.8: *riṇag rodhāṃsi kṛtrimāṇi* = 'he removed artificial barriers' makes this clear; *rodhas* means 'dam' elsewhere in the ṚV, as in later Sanskrit. Indra is praised for restoring to its natural course the river Vibālī, which had flooded land along its banks. That is, the Pre-Aryan method of agriculture depended upon natural floods and flooding the lands on the banks of smaller rivers by means of seasonal (RV. 5.32.2) dams (without regular masonry), to obtain the fertilising deposit of silt to be stirred by the harrow. The Aryans shattered this dam system, thereby ruining the agriculture of the region and the possibility of continuing city life for long, or of maintaining the urban population. The fact of the ruin is undeniable: the causes have to be deduced from whatever data is available, which includes numerous heavy flood silt deposits that are visible in Mohenjo-daro excavations. The very floods which endangered city and hamlet had made possible the agriculture which supported the inhabitants."[34]

Kosambi's theory of the agricultural technique in the Harappan region depending on a toothed harrow rather than plough has to be discarded, of course, after the excavation at Kalibangan revealed an actual ploughed field. However, at least among a section of archaeologists the "flood theory" is receiving increasing importance. If there is substance in this theory, it helps us to understand the Ṛgvedic passages related to Indra's exploit against Vṛtra—the snake-like obstructor of water—much better than the earlier views wanting us to read this or that myth in these passages. Archaeology thus becomes a significant tool for the interpretation of Ṛgvedic passages which remain otherwise more or less mysterious for us.

9. Summing Up

One reason for the tenacious objection against the theory of the Aryan invasion as the final cause of the already decaying Indus civilisation resulting from the cumulative effect of various possible causes seems to be frankly chauvinistic. Later Indian mythology wants to feed us with the belief that Indra was the king of the gods after all. Imputing to him such a negative activity as the destruction of the glorious civilisation of ancient India can understandably hurt the feelings of some, rooted primarily on religious convictions. An example of this seems to be the article on "The Myth of the Aryan Invasion of Harappan Towns" by K.M. Srivastava. After attempting to refute elaborately the theory of the Aryan invasion, he apparently feels the need of coming out sharply against Wheeler's statement that 'on circumstantial evidence, Indra stands condemned'. As already noted, Srivastava passionately proclaims:

"Indra, therefore, stands completely exonerated."

As against such a passionate defence of the Vedic god, at least one point needs to be remembered. The *Ṛgveda* is a collection of songs and hymns of an ancient period after all, and hence it will be an anachronism to judge the standard of morality reflected in it by our contemporary standards. Sacking or destroying the Harappan cities may appear more or less deplorable if judged by the moral standards of our time. But it was not so to the Vedic poets, who saw in such actions the most magnificent feat of courage and strength, and therefore, which, in their standard, must have been a highly laudable performance. That is why, they sang of the glory of Indra as *purandara* or destroyer of the cities. They would not have surely done it had they been under the influence of our standard of morality.

So the rather emotional statement completely exonerating Indra makes no real sense. To the ancient poets of the *Ṛgveda,* the personal bravery and strength of Indra was higly honourable, though these were often exhibited under the influence of alcohol or the intoxicating drink they called *soma.*

The point is that the standard of morality changes, not only from age to age but mainly because of the social conditions in which it is expressed. In the society in which the Vedic poets lived, certain acts considered most despicable by our standards of morality are actually praised by the poets in ways that appear to us to be most shocking. Here is an extreme example of this. In one hymn of the *Ṛgveda,* a certain poet praises Indra by way of addressing him as follows:

> Who has made thy mother a widow? Who has sought to slay the sleeping and the waking? What deity has been more gracious than thou, since thou hast slain the father having seized him by the foot? (RV. iv. 18.12)

We have—from the standpoint of our own sense of morality —perhaps no adequate vocabulary to condemn such an act of abject patricide, particularly when it is associated with the story that Indra did it because his father had stolen some amount of the intoxicating stuff from Indra's stock *(Taittirīya Saṃhitā* vi. 1.3.6), to which Sāyaṇa refers.

Can we, with our sense of morality, exonerate Indra from such an act? We cannot. But such a question would have perhaps made no sense to the Vedic poet himself.

Wheeler's use of the words "Indra stands condemned" was perhaps intended to be rhetorical, and surely some kind of plagiarism. But Srivastava's retort that "Indra stands completely exonerated" is *just Aryan chauvinism.*

REFERENCES

1. B. & R. Allchin RCIP 213.
2. V. Gordon Childe NLMAE 184-85.
3. A. Ghosh 83-84.
4. B. & R. Allchin RCIP 167.
5. D.K. Chakrabarti in EIP 205.
6. M.R. Mughal in ACI 91.
7. D.K. Chakarabrti in EIP 207.
8. B. & R. Allchin BIC 129 n.
9. B. & R. Allchin RCIP 213 ff.
10. D.D. Kosambi 59-60.
11. J. Marshall MIC I. *Preface* iv, emphasis added.
12. J. Needham GT 168-69, emphasis added.
13. *Ibid* 155-56.
14. V. Gordon Childe NLMAE 187.
15. R.E.M. Wheeler IC 127.
16. B. & R. Allchin RCIP 224 .
17. D.P. Agrawal AI 188 ff.
18. *Ibid* 191.
19. B. & R. Allchin RCIP 191.
20. R.E.M. Wheeler IC 126.
21. G.L. Possehl ACI 288.
22. B. & R. Allchin RCIP 43.
23. *Ibid* 225.
24. V. Gordon Childe WHH 128.
25. V. Gordon Childe NLMAE 187-88.
26. M. Wheeler reprinted in ACI 291.
27. G.F. Dales reprinted in ACI 293-96.
28. G.F. Dales in ACI 296.
29. K.M. Srivastava in FIC 441.
30. *Ibid* 442.
31. *Ibid*.
32. A.A. Macdonell VM 60.
33. *Ibid* 59.
34. D.D. Kosambi 70-71.

4

Vedic Religion : Myth and Reality

1. Preliminary Remarks

In 1963, Leonard Woolley observed: "The Aryan conquerors were a simple, not to say a barbarous people, pastoral nomads for the most part, some perhaps petty farmers who had not even a word for 'brick' in their vocabulary; they could destroy, but could not rebuild."[1]

From the viewpoint of material culture, there is no ground to question this observation, excepting of course an unwarranted veneration for the Vedas and for those who composed these. Archaeologists with a sense of objective coercion on them imposed by the actual material remains unearthed wanted to look at the period of over a thousand years following the final destruction of the Harappan culture as the Dark Age or Dark Period, because nothing substantial was known about it even a few decades ago. Thanks to the brisk fieldwork of Indian archaeologists in recent years, we have now ampler information about this period than we had at the time of Indian independence.

In spite of this, however, the period continues to be "dark" after all, i.e. from the viewpoint of material culture. It was according to some, indicative of the beginning of the iron age. But R.S. Sharma, reviewing the relevant evidences, rightly observes, "till the sixth century B.C. northern India did not enter into a full-fledged iron age".[2] This means that the time-gap between the final decline of Harappan Civilisation and the beginning of the real iron age is over a thousand years, because on the basis of the radio-carbon dating of D.P. Agrawal it is difficult to doubt today that the former, i.e. the end of Harappan Civilisation, took place in about 1750 B.C. This intervening period of over a thousand years is the Dark Age of our archaeologists, because it is a period of an almost all round technological regression. Then slowly began the reintroduction of urban life, which , as compared to Harappan Culture, is often called the period of second urbanisation. As A. Ghosh puts it, "For her next cities, her 'second urbanisation', India had to wait for over a thousand years after the disappearance of the Indus cities—till the middle of the sixth century B.C. which saw simultaneously the beginnings of her historical period".[3] By this time, the invading Vedic people—who called themselves the *arya*-s or Aryans—had at least substantially lost their racial identity and got mingled with the local people, or as A. Ghosh very aptly puts it, "the early Aryan society had made room for the Indian society, in which it is difficult to isolate Aryan and non-Aryan elements."[4]

2. The Veda

There is thus an obvious truth in the observation of Leonard Woolley with which we began this lecture. What needs to be added to it, however, is that this truth is strictly confined to the viewpoint of material culture. From another viewpoint, however, the same Vedic people *created* something that continues to be a wonder of wonders. It consists of a vast store of songs and poems—often mentioned as "hymns"—over a thousand of which survive for us in the form of the vast collection called the *Ṛgveda-saṃhitā*. The codification of this took place many centuries later, for the composers of the songs were really pre-literate people. The songs or "hymns" were originally composed and were yet preserved meticulously by the most amazing form of sheer retentive memory without affecting even their original accents. This by itself indicates how much of importance was imputed to the songs by the Vedic people themselves. But Hindu orthodoxy—or at least a very dominant section thereof—usually goes to an extreme extent, when, without bothering to actually read or understand the real nature of these songs, proclaims that these are but repositories of the highest spiritual wisdom, revealed to the "poets" *(kavi-s)* or "seers" thereof. It is even proclaimed that these songs were too holy to be read—or even listened to—by the low-caste people and women, leading Marx to come out with the sarcastic remark: "the Indian Brahmin... proves the holiness of the Vedas by reserving for himself alone the right to read it."[5]

Marx was not, of course, a specialist in the Vedas, nor apparently was he aware of the fact that practically a microscopic minority of the Brahmins have actually the patience or diligence for really reading the Veda. For the vast majority of the Brahmins, who make a living of the professed spiritual wisdom of the Veda and who go to the extent of claiming that the Veda is the basic plank of Hindu religion, the word Veda is practically nothing more than sales talk or a political slogan to justify their privileges. Exsperated by all these, one of our foremost scholars, MM. H.P. Sastri, while writing an essay on the Veda, remarks that those who are Sanskritists by profession though without ever actually caring to read the Veda, may as well spare themselves the trouble to read his essay.

Since, the basic points that I want to make about the *Ṛgveda* are already made by Mahamahopadhyaya Hara Prasad Sastri and this with an authority many times more than I can possibly have, it may be wiser for me to allow him to speak on these instead of trying to speak myself. In short, I propose to quote here extensively from his exquisitely charming essay on the Veda, written originally in Bengali. I shall have to make a rough English rendering of it with full awareness, of course, that such a rendering is bound to miss much of his original sarcasm and his power of persuasion.

Before quoting him, however, I may mention one point. As most of you are aware, in 1885-87 was first published in Bengali the translation of the whole of the *Ṛgveda*: the translation appears to be as literal as it is perhaps possible and as translator, it bore the name of Ramesh Chandra Dutta. Though famous as a civilian as well as a pioneer worker on the economic history of India, Ramesh Chandra Dutta was not a Sanskritist—at least not essentially so. He could not translate the *Ṛgveda* on his own—a task that required a great deal of mastery of the Sanskrit language, specially the archaic Sanskrit in which the *Ṛgveda* was composed. It was therefore necessary for him to depend on the help of a very competent Sanskritist.

But there was then a formidable difficulty about getting one. Sanskritic studies were in those days mainly confined to the Brahmins, most of whom believed that only the Brahmins were entitled to Vedic studies. R.C. Dutta was by birth not a Brahmin and it appears that the orthodox Brahmin community then frowned upon the idea of a non-Brahmin meddling with the Vedas. What then could he do?

He appealed to Pandit Isvara Chandra Vidyasagara for help, who was already waging a veritable war against the obnoxious aspects of Brahmanical orthodoxy, though with a far greater mastery of the Sanskrit language than most of the orthodox Brahmins professed. From the preface to Dutta's translation of the *Ṛgveda* it appears that Vidyasagar readily moved forward to offer the assistance required. Apparently, Vidyasagar himself was then too busy with many things to take part in the stupendous task of helping Dutta to translate the whole of the *Ṛgveda*. Fortunately, however, among his own students there was then a young one who had already acquired a superb mastery of the Sanskrit language. He was Hara Prasad Sastri. So Vidyasagar sent H.P. Sastri to help Ramesh Chandra Dutta, and H.P. Sastri—himself fully free from the repelling aspects of the Brahmanical orthodoxy—moved forward to take up the arduous taks of explaining to Dutta the literal meaning of the entire *Ṛgveda*, freely depending, of course, on the commentary by Sāyaṇa. Thus was made possible the Bengali version of the entire *Ṛgveda* which eventually came out as having been translated by

R.C. Dutta. I have myself often wondered how much of it incorporates the work of H.P. Sastri, specially because of the exquisite charms of simple and direct prose in which the Bengali *Ṛgveda* came out—a literary style often reminding us of Hara Prasad Sastri.

I have mentioned all this specially to clarify one point. The long extract from H.P. Sastri's essay which we are going to use here may appear to be objectionable—even atrocious to many of our conservative readers. Let them not forget, however, that this essay was not written only with a smattering knowledge of the Veda. It was written instead on the basis of a detailed mastery of the whole of the *Ṛgveda*—a phenomenon which is rare and is becoming increasingly rarer these days. It is thus not easy to brush aside his observations, except of course on the strength of an ignorance about the Veda.

With this preliminary clarification, we proceed to quote H.P. Sastri who opens the essay with a biting satire on the orthodox way of looking back at the Veda. H.P. Sastri observes:

> The very name Veda evokes in every Indian an emotion of overwhelming awe: One is a rare-born who reads the Veda and one who understands it is a veritable incarnation of Śiva or Viṣṇu. Purity of body and mind is the precondition of Vedic study, which brings the power of achieving the impossible with the help of the spells. Viśwāmitra utters the spell, and lo, after a drought of twelve long years there comes rain in torrents. I utter a spell here and my enemy in Delhi is annihilated. With Vedic spells, the barren becomes mother, the sick cured, the poor prosperous and the dying man back to life. When you are in need of any proof, just claim that it is declared in the Veda and none will dare to contradict you. Such indeed are the ideas of the ignorant; the Veda is a miracle and a miracle-maker; it is inscrutable, unreadable, un-understandable, unapproachable. Without the grace of the goddess of learning and the accumulated merit of the pious acts of the previous births, none can have an access to the Veda.

But what exactly is the Veda? It is nothing but an anthology of some poems, songs, etc., composed by various gifted poets in different times, under diverse conditions and with various purposes. While trying to explain this, we hope that it would kindly be skipped ever by those that have high things to say about Sanskrit as a mere matter of profession and therefore who, without ever bothering to read the Veda, only know that it is composed by the God Brahmā. Actually speaking, this literature is somewhat like Palgrave's *Golden Treasury of Songs and Lyrics,* an anthology of songs and poems of many a gifted poet... An anthology of songs is of course merely an anthology; but how could the Veda being essentially so, acquire such a stupendous influence on religion? What explains this veneration for the Veda over hundreds of years?

The great antiquity of the Veda is about the main reason for this. Of all the books in the world, the Veda is surely the oldest. Moreover, for purposes of knowing anything about the age in which it was composed, we have only the Veda to depend upon... Let us imagine a situation in which after a lapse of about 3000 years all the books written by the Englishmen become extinct, leaving only the *Golden Treasury,* to survive. In such circumstances, the *Golden Treasury,* too, is likely to acquire a similar importance. It alone would then tell us about the thoughts, poetic capabilities and the social customs of the Englishmen.

The historian and the archaeologist will of course concentrate on the great antiquity and historical value of the Veda. From the poet's point of view, however, there is no other poetry in the world that can be easily compared to the Veda. The Veda is not an epic of the Homerian type; yet each poem *(sūkta)* of the Veda is an epic in its own way. It was then only the childhood of mankind and there could then be nothing to compare to the tremendous power man has acquired today on the external world.

In these circumstances, everything—fire, air, cloud, thunder, lightning, storm—appeared to the poets to be variable gods. It needs a great deal of development of abstract thinking to arrive at the conception of the presiding deities; men in their childhood were yet to develop it. They saw everything with the child's eyes, pictured everything with brightest hues. Their eyes were the eyes of the poets. At the same time the knowledge, the labour and the mastery over the external world which the composition of Homer's enormous poem presupposes were not possessed by them. They could just express the depths of their hearts, their awe and fear, their apprehension, hope and aspiration. And how did they express all these? There was nothing artificially clever, nothing deliberately thought out, nothing laboured about their expressions. Whenever they felt any fear or awe, it soon occupied the whole of their inner being. And they immediately expressed it in words. The words, like the feelings, were simple, clear and noble. There was no burden of the rhetoric, no anxiety to conceal anything or to discriminate between good and bad taste, no calculated contrivance for purposes of appealing to others. Their expressions had the same nobility as their feelings... Whatever they looked at appeared to them to be colossal, wonderful and a marvel. A hillock would have thrilled them a hundred times more than the great Himalayas thrill us today. Lest it upset the social norm, we refuse sometimes to express what we feel; these poets expressed the same feelings in a higly magnified yet simple language. They were poets, because they were full of that sense of wonder which is the universal characteristic of the poet's heart. Yet, compared to them, our poets today are but dry men of affairs.

Nevertheless, the Veda is regarded above all as a religious work... How was it that for thousands of years it was worshipped by millions of people? How could some poems and songs eventually acquire this scriptural status? It will be a folly to suggest that people were just fools to have imagined this. Really speaking, the process is indicative of some important psychological truth. Those who composed these songs believed that they could do it because of some kind of direct vision, which these days we call inspiration. Their fellowmen, too, believed that the composers worked under supernatural inspiration. Let us suppose that you are a poet while I am not and the two of us stay together. With your strong imagination you see everything as full of beauty; being not a poet I see the earth just as it is, the sky merely as the sky. Here lies the difference between the two of us. We know this to be a

> difference resulting from our different mental make-up. But people then were not aware of this. They could only note that when the poet sang he experienced a peculiar inner unrest which was not normally felt by him. How was this unrest to be accounted for? Accustomed as he was to see gods everywhere, the poet saw in this, too, the working of god. So he said, 'God has worked me up like this'. And the other wondered: Since he can do what we cannot, he must have been aided by god... In the course of time, the names of the poets who actually composed these songs were forgotten and the deities imagined to have helped the poets came to be known as the real inspirers of the Veda. This led Mādhavācārya to claim that a *ṛṣi* (Vedic poet) was one who saw the *mantra, the root ṛṣ* meaning 'to see'. It was because of this, again, that Bhavabhuti was somewhat annoyed with Kālidāsa's use of the word *mantrakṛt* ('the maker of *mantra*'); instead of *mantrakṛtām* he said, the word should rather be *mantradṛśām;* the *ṛṣis* never made the *mantras,* they merely saw them. Eventually, with the final supremacy of monotheism in the Brahmanical religion, the authorship of the Veda was attributed to the Supreme God. God being eternal, the Veda, too, was considered eternal. Being the work of God, the Veda can contain no error; it is all-truth, all-holy, all-illumination. Thus it was that a collection of simple songs acquired the scriptural status....
>
> In the Vedic age, however, people were very simple and straightforward. It is extremely difficult for us to enter their mental world. We should be able to understand the Veda much better if we can project ourselves in imagination into the Vedic world. We should then have some real idea of the activities and the sociology of those days and should understand a lot of what the poets had to say. But it is not easy to enter that world. For this purpose, it is necessary to know a great deal about the ancient world and about the mental make-up of the ancient people. It is not enough to know only about India; it is also necessary to know the history of the ancient world wherever the Aryans appeared.[6]

All this—particularly the secular or near-secular view of the Veda as but a compilation of primitive poetry—will undoubtedly be outrageous for Indian orthodoxy, not to mention anything of some modern people organising a Vedic University somewhere in Switzerland wanting to prove that the Vedic "seers" intuitively anticipated what is latest in modern science. But there is no substance in it at all. In substantiation of H.P. Sastri's view, we shall rather quote in rough English rendering some of the actual songs or "hymns" from the *Ṛgveda* and try to show how the Vedic poets themselves were in close friendly terms with their own "deities", so that the "sense of the holy" which we are accustomed to imagine separates man from God, was practically unknown to the Vedic poets themselves. We shall next discuss the point that H.P. Sastri seems to skip over, namely the manipulation of our law makers and also of a great medieval politician that actually went to the making of the later awesome view of the Veda. Lastly, we shall try to discuss the most tricky point, namely why, in spite of the great veneration for the Veda, the Vedic gods had really no future even in the religious history of India.

Some specimens from the *Ṛgveda* first. It is really questionable how far any religious sentiment or spiritual value in our sense is at all to be found in the genuinely older portions of the *Ṛgveda*. There is no doubt that the hymns and songs are full of extravagant praise for all sorts of deities or *devas*. But they are often crassly human heroes, looting food and cattle for the tribesmen and sharing these out among themselves; sitting with them in their assemblies and addressed by them in endearing terms like 'friends' or 'the best of friends',—often simple natural phenomena and inanimate objects even like the hill (*parvata*), the herb *(oṣadhi)*, the tree *(vanaspati)*, the forests *(araṇyānī)*, the weapons *(āyudha)* like the bow and arrow. Sometimes, again, the deities are just the embodiments of fulfilment of purely this-worldly desires, like 'the protection against abortion',[7] 'the protection against consumptive diseases',[8] the protection against the nightmare'.[9] A fascinating deity of this kind is Pitu, i.e. food. The barbarian poets with their healthy appetite praised him for being savoury and delicious and because he 'makes the body fat';. In the general context of all sorts of traditional and modern claims attributing the highest spiritual wisdom to the *Ṛgveda*, this hymn to Pitu or food may be quoted here for its obvious interest.

Ṛ.V. I. 187. Deity Pitu or Food. Poet Agastya

> I glorify Food, the Great, the Upholder, the Strong, by whose invigorating power Tṛta (the famous) tortured the deformed Vṛtra. Savoury Food, honeyed Food, we welcome thee; become our protector. Come to us, beneficial Food, a source of delight, a friend well-respected, and having no envy. Your flavours, Food, are diffused through the regions, as the winds are spread through the sky. These (men), oh Food, who are your distributors, most sweet Food, they who are the eaters of our and your juices, they increase like you with elongating necks. The minds of the mighty gods are fixed, oh Food, upon you; by your active assistance (Indra) slew Ahi. Oh Food, the wealth which is associated with the mountains went to you; hear you, Oh sweet one, be accessible to our eating. And since we enjoy the abundance of the waters and the plants;—Therefore, Oh body, may thou grow fat, and since we enjoy, Soma, thy mixture with boiled milk or boiled barley;— therefore, Oh body, may thou grow fat....[10] And so on.

The refrain deserves special notice: 'Oh, body, may thou grow fat'—*vātāpe pīvaḥ it bhava.*

It is true, of course, that Pitu or food does not in any way rank among the major Vedic gods. As doubtless, again, is the fact that Indra is one. Here is a delightful drunken monologue of Indra, with the refrain that he had taken many draughts of the heady drink called Soma. As the world's earliest poem of drunkenness, it obviously has a great historical interest, though even the most extravagant theology can hardly extract any religious sentiment in our sense out of it.

Ṛgveda X. 119. Deity Indra. Poet Lava, the Son of Indra

> By temper I am one who gifts cows and horses; I have drunk Soma in many draughts. As winds shake and elongate the tree, so also Soma—having been drunk by me—shakes and

> elongates me. I have drunk Soma in many draughts. As the fast-moving horses make the chariot fast-moving so also Soma—having been taken by me—makes me move fast. I have drunk Soma in many draughts. As the cow moves towards the calf lowing, so are the hymns coming towards me. I have taken Soma in many draughts. As the carpenter constructs the upper part of the chariot, so have I mentally constructed the hymns. I have drunk Soma in many draughts. No man of the five classes *(pañcakṛṣṭi)* can elude my eyes. I have taken Soma in many draughts. Heaven and earth—the two taken together cannot equate even one side of mine. I have taken Soma in many draughts. My glory overflows heaven as well as this vast earth. I have taken Soma in many draughts. Lo, I will place this earth (where I will), either here or there. I have taken Soma in many draughts. I can burn this whole earth and I can destroy any place that you may name. I have taken Soma in many draughts. One part of mine is in heaven and another scratching the earth below. I have taken Soma in many draughts. I am greater than the great, I have risen towards the sky. I have taken Soma in many draughts. Receiving the offering I go, graced by hymns, carrying the oblation to the gods. I have taken Soma in many draughts.

The megalomania of the drunken god is, of course, easily understood. If you take so many draughts of the heady drink today, you are likely to be a megalomaniac. What is not so easily understood, however, in the standard of our moral values is the glorification of it in Vedic imagination. But that is only to be expected. The Vedic poets were not—and could not be—inhibited by our sense of morality and even of decency. They marvelled instead at the heroic performances of Indra, often under the influence of the drink. One of the poets went so far as to express the desire of Soma normally flowing to Indra—as normally indeed as the male genital moves to the hairy triangular organ of the female (RV. ix. 112.4). Would the great admirers of Vedic religion try to dig some religious sentiment in our sense in this? If so, they would also be obliged to flout what actually comes down to us as the *Ṛgveda*, i.e. at least its plain meaning.

It may not be irrelevant to quote here a comment of Winternitz which is likely to be far more helpful for our understanding of the Ṛgvedic mentality than heaps of theology sought to be dumped upon this primitive poetry. As he observes:

> However, we must not form too exalted an idea of the moral conditions in ancient India, and not picture these to ourselves in such an idyllic manner, as certainly Max Müller has at times done. We hear in the hymns of the *Rig Veda* of incest, seduction, conjugal unfaithfulness, the procuring of abortion, as also of deception, theft and robbery. All this, however, proves nothing against the antiquity of the *Rig Veda*. Modern ethnology knows nothing of the 'unspoiled children of nature' any more than it regards all primitive people as rough savages or cannibal monsters. The ethnologist knows that a step-ladder of endless gradations of the most widely differing cultural conditions leads from the primitive people to the half-civilised people, and right up to the civilised nations. We need not, therefore, imagine the people of the *Rig Veda* either as an innocent shepherd people, or as a horde of rough savages, nor, on the other hand, as a people of ultra-refined culture. The picture of culture which is unfolded in these songs, shows us the Aryan Indians as an active, joyful and war-like people, of simple, and still partly savage habits. The Vedic singers implore the gods for help against the enemy, for victory in battle, for glory and rich booty; they pray for wealth, heaps of gold and countless herds of cattle, for rain for their fields, for the blessing of children, and long life. As yet we do not find in the songs of the *Rig Veda* that effeminate, ascetic and pessimistic trait of the Indian character with which we shall meet again and again in later Indian literature.

3. Gods and Men: The Religious Sentiment

What is said above about the moral sentiments seems to be true also about the religious sentiments at least to a great extent. In spite of the *Ṛgveda* being crowded with a whole host of what are called the gods and demi-gods, it is really questionable if we are at all permitted to read in this vast literature religious sentiments in our sense. There are perhaps many ways in which this can be illustrated. We propose to choose in our next lecture one of these, namely the relation of god and man in the *Ṛgveda*, where the line of demarcation between the two often appears to be at best a thin one. I have quoted a fairly large number of examples of this in my book *Lokayata*.[10] Since, however, these are vital for the present discussion, I may as well reiterate some of these.

Indra is invoked simply as 'man': "I invoke Indra, the man (*naram*), who fulfils the desires of many from his ancient dwellings—in the same manner as my ancestors did in the past." (i.30.9). Agni is said to be *nṛvatsakhā sabhāvān*—a friend of the most human type and a member of the tribal assembly (iv. 2.5). Indra and Agni knew the ancient sages Kaṇva, Atri, Manu, 'who were skilled and who had an abode among the gods' (i. 139.9). The ancient seers sat in joyful company with the *devāḥ* and with true spells (*mantras*) generated Uṣas (vii. 76.4). Indra is praised as the chief among men (*nṛtamaḥ*) and one who shares out wealth (*vibhaktā*) along with other human beings (*nṛbhiḥ śākaiḥ*) (iv. 17.11). We shall return later to discuss the extremely interesting implication of the word *vibhaktā* or apportioner. For the present, the incomplete dehumanisation of the Vedic gods.

Agni is addressed as the chief human being among the human beings (*nṛṇāṃ nṛtamaḥ*) (i. 77.4), the chief among men (*nṛṇāṃ nṛpate*) (ii. 1.1), the best of men (*nṛtamaḥ*) (v.4.6). He is invoked to produce (*bṛhat kṛdhi*), like the human being (*nṛvat*), food in large quantity among human beings (*nṛṇāṃ*) (v. 18.5). Like the human being, says another *ṛk* addressed to him, he gives us wealth and cattle to our sons and grandsons (vi. 1.12). Mitra and Varuṇa are invoked to come and join the soma-drinking in the company of human beings (i.137.3). May Indra and Viṣṇu like human beings, give us houses (iv. 55. 4). Aśvins, along with Agastya, are said to be the foremost among the leading men (i. 180.8).

The epithet of being the chief man among men is, however, most frequently used in the case of Indra. He is the finest man among all human beings (*nṛṇāṃ nṛtamam*) (iii.51.4). Along with other humans he wins battles, and, in their company, he eats good food (i. 178.3). The Yajamānas (financiers of the ritual) are asked to offer cakes to Indra, who is immediately present and is the bravest of the human beings (*nṛṇāṃ vīratamāya*) (iii. 52.8). As foremost among men (*nṛṇāṃ nṛtama*) he cuts the enemies to pieces in battles (iv. 33.3). We shall prepare *soma* for Indra, who is.... the best man among men (*nare naryāya nṛtamāya nṛṇāṃ*) (iv. 25.4). He is the strongest leader among men (*saviṣṭhaṃ nṛṇāṃ naram*) (viii. 40. 2). In the past, he was the chief among men (*purā cit śūra nṛṇāṃ*) (viii.66.5). As the chief of men he rends asunder the clouds and causes showers (iv. 22.2). As the chief of the human beings, again, he has similar dwellings as of the other human beings (*mānuṣāṇām sam okaḥ nṛtamaḥ*) (vi. 18.7). He even speaks like human beings (*nṛvat vadan*) and 'comes to us and gives us food' (x.28.12). Like a human being he entered the army of the opponent (iii. 34.5). Shouting like a human being (*nṛvat nonuvanta*) he made the wind blow (iv. 22.4). Like a human being, again, he increased the strength (vi.19.1). Indra, who is like a human being, from thee do we—along with the leaders of men—desire wealth (vi. 19.10). In the matter of food-procuring, Indra is the chief among men: the *ṛk* in which this occurs runs as a refrain in the third book of the *Ṛgveda*, being the last *ṛk* of no less than twelve *sūktas* (30-32, 34-36, 38, 39, 43, 48-50) and it reoccurs twice in the tenth book (x. 89.18). Presumably, the Vedic poets attached great significance to this. In another *ṛk*, Indra is said to be not only the chief among the human beings, (*nṛṇāṃ nṛtamaḥ*) but also as 'common' among (equal to?) them (*naryaḥ*) (x. 29.1). With all these evidences, is it not safe to presume that Indra was originally only the culture-hero of some Vedic tribe, and the word *deva* originally meant only this? It is after all a postulate of comparative philology that words change more slowly than the meanings attached to them.

This conclusion will be strongly challenged by our orthodox scholars. But to them we may answer that we have in the writings of no less an orthodox commentator than Sāyaṇa himself, the rather startling admission that during the composition of the *Ṛgveda,* actual human beings were really being raised to the status of Vedic deities. The evidence is as follows. In one *ṛk* Indra is addressed as the killer in great battles and the increaser of human skill with the assistance of other human beings. But the context in which this occurs suggests that Indra was doing all this with the assistance rather of the Maruts. This naturally presented a problem to Sāyaṇa: How could the human beings of the *ṛk* mean the Maruts as well? And he answered, 'by the human beings are meant the men who, though originally men, later attained the status of the gods and were called the Maruts' (*nṛbhiḥ manuṣyaiḥ eva sadbhiḥ paścāt devatvam āpannaiḥ marudbhiḥ)* (Sāyaṇa on i. 129. 2).

This explanation is provocative and the temptation to digress slightly cannot be helped. If Sāyaṇa was here true to the Vedic tradition, then the attainment of godhead on the part of the Maruts may be looked upon as part of the living memory of the Ṛgvedic poets. And if this be true, it should be possible for us to infer the original human characteristics of the Maruts by examining the characteristics attributed to them in the *Ṛgveda,* though as gods. The special significance of this lies in the circumstance that of all the Vedic deities the Maruts alone retained the strongest marks of the primitive group-life. They were most frequently referred to as living in *gaṇa* or the tribal collectivity. They were all brothers among themselves and strict equality was believed to exist among them. They grew up together, were born at the same place, and had the same abode. They were strictly of one strength, one friendship and one birth. (i. 14.3; iii 35.9; etc.; i. 165.1; v.59.6; etc.; v. 56.5; v. 53.1; vii. 56.1; etc.)

Thus the Maruts had this special importance in the *Ṛgveda* that they retained the relics of not only a distinct history of human origin but also of the communistic or pre-class society to which, as human beings, they must have originally belonged.

The human origin of the Vedic deities is not confined to the case of Maruts. Sāyaṇa said that the Ṛbhus, too, originally human beings, were eventually raised to the status of gods. This genealogy of the Ṛbhus is not indeed an invention of Sāyaṇa. For in the Ṛgveda itself (i.110.4) we come across the startling declaration that the Ṛbhus, being yet mortal, attained immortality (*martāsaḥ santaḥ amṛtatvam ānaśuḥ*). Sāyaṇa said practically the same thing about the Vahnis—*pūrvam manuṣyatvena maraṇayogyāḥ api amṛtatva-lābhena prāṇān dhāritavantaḥ:* though previously, being human beings, they were mortal yet they later became immortal (on 1.20.8). Of course, as deities, they were only minor in importance. But the Aśvins were not so. And the Ṛgveda itself distinctly referred to the Aśvins being raised to the status of the gods (*devāḥ bhavathe*). (iii.54.17.)

Significantly enough, even after attaining the godhead, the Ṛbhus retained very clear relics of the collective life. As Sāyaṇa pointed out, in the Ṛgveda the Ṛbhus were addressed in the singular (*janmane*) because they formed a collective body *(saṁgha)*. And the Aśvins themselves maintained equality and a comradely relationship with the human beings:

> O Aśvins, our friendship with you comes down from our fathers; in friendship you are equal with us; know your and our grandfather to be the same;. (*yuvoḥ hi naḥ sakhyā pitryāṇi samānaḥ bandhuḥ uta tasya vittam:* the interpretation of *bandhuḥ* is after Sāyaṇa). (vii. 72.2).

What needs to be noted is that the Vedic poets felt this essentially friendly and human relationship also for their other important deities. Here are a few, though not very carefully chosen, examples:

Indra was a friend indeed! He was a friend with friends; the friend and benefactor and protector. (i.63.4) He was a friend coming from the heaven and honouring 'us' as his friends (i. 63.4); a friend accompanied by faithful friends (iii. 39.5); listening as a friend to the praises of his friends. (iii. 43.4). The friends of Indra poured out *Soma* for him (iii. 30.1).

Such examples are, however, too few to give us any real idea of how persistently Indra—described as 'the most human of the gods.... whom the seers most closely fashioned in their own likeness'—was addressed or invoked as a friend. For such references in the Ṛgveda are really numerous and it would be tedious to quote them all. Nevertheless, we may mention here one more *ṛk* because, over and above expressing the intensely friendly relation felt by the Vedic poets for Indra, it has, in distinctly referring to the past, some additional interest for us. 'O Indra, the giver of horses, cows, barley, wealth, as you were our wish-yielder in the past, so are you our friend and speak to us who are your friends'. (i.53.2)

Agni again was like a father, friendship with whom was the best of friendship (*sakhā sakhye vareṇyaḥ*) (i. 26.3), a friend of all peoples (*jāmiḥ janānām*) and the most praiseworthy friend among all friends (*sakhā sakhibhyaḥ īḍyaḥ*) (1.75.4). He was friend and minister and well disposed towards friends. The seers, desiring protection, called themselves his friends. 'Be favourably disposed, O Agni, on approaching us; the fulfiller like a friend or the parents; since men (enemies) are the grievous oppressors of men, do thou consume the foes who come against us.' And so on. (iii. 14. ; iii. 9.1; iii. 18.1) Indeed, the references to such extremely friendly relations to Agni in the Ṛgveda are no less numerous than those to Indra.

The Viśvadeva-s (all-gods) were addressed as comrades (iii. 29.4). This comradeship, coming down from the days of the fathers, was felt to be immensely old (iii. 54.9). Similar must have been the relationship felt by the Vedic poets for Aśvins: it was desired that the ancient comradeship with them be revived and the friendship be sealed with drinks, being delighted together on the basis of equality (*punaḥ purāṇam sakhyam kṛṇvānāḥ sakhyā madhvā madema saha nu samānāḥ*) (iii. 58.6). Again, Soma, Brahmaṇaspati, Savitṛ, Varuṇa, Mitra and Aryaman and others all maintained warm and comradely relations with the Vedic poets and their kinsmen. However, as comrades, Varuṇa, Mitra and Aryaman were the foremost. Macdonell observed:

> Aryaman though mentioned about a hundred times in the Ṛgveda is so destitute of individual characteristics, that in the *Naighaṇṭuka* he is passed over in the list of gods. Except in two passages, he is always mentioned with other deities, in the great majority of cases with Mitra and Varuṇa. In less than a dozen passages the word has only the appellative senses of 'comrade' and 'groomsman', which are occasionally also connected with the god. Thus Agni is once addressed with the words: 'Thou art *aryaman* when (the wooer) of maiden'. The derivative adjective *aryamya* 'relating to a comrade', once occurs as a parallel to *mitrya*, 'relating to a friend'. Thus the conception of Aryaman seems to have differed but little from that of the greater Āditya Mitra, 'the friend'. The name goes back to the Indo-Iranian period , as it occurs in the *Avesta*.[11]

Similarly, Varuṇa, observed Macdonell, was 'on a footing of friendship with his worshipper.'[12] How far the word 'worshipper' correctly describes the relation of the Vedic poets and their kinsmen to the Vedic gods needs really to be settled. For the present, however, we may examine an important indication—a clear and distinct reference to a past involved in this comradely mention of Varuṇa:

> What has become of our friendship with you, which was in the ancient days, without any spite? May we foster it and enter your thousand-door abode—you who are full of food. (vii. 88.5)

This reference to the past has some special significance with regard to the specific history of Varuṇa. It has also some general significance in the Ṛgveda, which we shall later take up.

The point is that 'some hundreds of years must have been needed for all the hymns found in the *Ṛgveda* to come into being'. There is no basis to think that during these hundreds of years the life and thought of the Vedic people remained unchanged. Therefore, it is only natural that the *Ṛgveda* should contain different strata of the thought reflecting also the fact of the Vedic people passing through different stages of social development. We have already before us theories concerning the different strata of the Ṛgveda as worked out by the foremost of the modern scholars. However, such theories, being based mostly on bare philological considerations, are liable to suffer from the limitation of a formal approach and may mislead us to expect a view of the earlier condition of the Vedic people only in the hymns actually composed earlier. On the other hand, the possibility remains that a hymn, even when considered later on linguistic grounds, may, nevertheless, by invoking the memory of the past, reveal something about the Vedic people during their comparatively early stage of social development. It is in such references to the past that we often come across the mention of the comradely relations of the Vedic poets with their gods, particularly Varuṇa. From these we may infer that the more we penetrate into the pre-history of the Vedic people, the clearer do we see their gods to be outspokenly human and maintaining a comradely relationship with the members of the tribe.

Philological considerations, too, corroborate this. Here is a *ṛk* of immense significance:

> O Agni, O Asura, this ritual (*yajña*) of ours is full of cows, of sheep (*avimāṅ*), of horses, of food, of offspring; may thou be always without anger being in our assembly (*sabhāvān*), a friend, like a human being (*nṛvat-sakhā*), possessing huge wealth and vast waters (iv.2.5).

Agni being addressed as an *asura* is indeed remarkable; Sāyaṇa found it too inconvenient to comment upon. It indicates that the *ṛk* dates back to a period when to the poets of the *Ṛgveda* the word *asura* had not fallen into disrepute. Probably, more significant than this is the use of the word *avimāṅ*, 'one full of sheep.' This is the solitary use of the word in the whole of the *Ṛgveda*, the only reference to the sheep as a form of wealth. This again indicates that the *ṛk* dates back to a period when the Vedic seers were still raising and tending the sheep, a practice they must have eventually given up. These, therefore, are evidences of the *ṛk* belonging to the most archaic stratum of the *Ṛgveda*. And it is also the *ṛk* in which the word *nṛvatsakhā*, 'friend-like-a-human being', occurs; in the comparatively earlier periods, the comradely relations felt by the Vedic poets for their gods were indeed overtly human.

Speaking of comradely relations, we are reminded here of a rather interesting evidence of Vedic literature. In the *Ṛgveda*, one of the words used for 'comrade' is *'jāmiḥ'*: Agni was addressed as *janānām jāmiḥ* (i.75.4), the comrade of all men. Sāyaṇa, on the authority of the *Uṇādi Sūtra* explained the word as follows: *jama adane jamanti saha ekasmin pātre adanti iti jāmavaḥ, bandhavaḥ:* 'The root *jam* means to eat: those who eat together from the same plate are friends, *jāmayaḥ*.' One point is clear: the word for comrade (*jāmiḥ*) is derived from the circumstance of having eaten from the same plate. The association of the word comrade with communism is indeed very old.

To sum up our present point: How much of divinity or godhood in our sense is to be imputed to these Vedic gods? From the plain meaning of the Vedic verses the answer is that it cannot be much. And if that is so, religious sentiment as we understand it is hardly to be read in the *Ṛgveda*. However, there is a strong tendency among the followers of Vedic orthodoxy claiming that the Veda is too holy to be understood according to its plain meaning. We now pass on to see what fate awaited the Vedic gods as the result of the final development of this tendency.

4. Claim of Ritual Use (Viniyoga) of All Vedic Verses

The *Ṛgveda* apart, three other compilations come down to us claiming the general title *Veda*. These are *Sāmaveda*, *Yajurveda* and *Atharvaveda*. Of these, the last had to await long to be admitted to the status of the Veda: the word usually used as referring to the Vedas in the ancient sources is *trayi* or "the three", i.e. as excluding the *Atharvaveda*. The *Sāmaveda*, again, has hardly the status of an independent Veda, it being but an anthology of the songs of the *Ṛgveda* selected with an eye to their melody value. Among the other Vedas thus we are left only with the *Yajurveda,* which we are told, had once a rather fabulous number of different recensions though of these only a few actually survive today.

That the *Yajurveda* came into being much later than the *Ṛgveda* can hardly be doubted. Also palpable is the fact of the drastic change in its main theme: the be-all and end-all of the *Yajurveda* are the *yajña*-s which are usually translated as the Vedic "sacrifices", though these are generally nothing more than primitive magical rituals, often enlarged or magnified to make them look most awe-inspiring, so that the rich patrons financing for these (called *Yajamāna*-s) may be induced to part with substantial "fees" or *dakṣiṇā*-s to the varieties of priests looking after the execution of its various aspects—priests who had no other ostensible means of their own subsistence, and hence from the social viewpoint were no more than parasites. If the *yajña*-s are the be-all and end-all of the *Yajurveda,* the *dakṣiṇā*-s are so for the Vedic priests.

With these points in mind, we may pass on to a view, a powerful exponent of which was Sāyaṇa, whose stature as the commentator of the Veda often tends to obscure the fact of his also having been a powerful politician of the fourteenth century A.D. He was a very influential minister of the Vijayanagara Empire, though after retiring from the post he became the *mahānta* or Head Abbot of one of the monasteries founded by Śaṃkara.

In his introduction to the commentary on the *Ṛgveda* Śayaṇa came out with the categorical claim that all the verses in the *Ṛgveda* were intended to be but *mantra*-s or incantations for the *yajña*-s of the *Yajurveda* and hence the *Yajurveda* is the basic plank of the entire Vedic literature. The Ṛgvedic verses were thus nothing if not having a *viniyoga* or application in the Vedic *yajña*-s.

The claim is in fact so utterly absurd that it hardly deserves any serious discussion. Not that there is no quotation from *Ṛgveda* in the ritual discussions of the *Yajurveda.* What these actually are, however, are only certain scraps from the *Ṛgvedic* verses, torn out of their actual contexts and, as Keith has shown, not necessarily free from corruption or misreading. What is worse, there is often no rhyme or reason connecting such scraps with the theme of the ritual—or of the part thereof—the injunctions for which are given in the *Yajurveda*. In any case, nobody has been able to show that the *entire Ṛgveda* was actually intended to be employed in the Vedic sacrifices and this because of the simple reason that it is impossible to do it. In short, Sāyaṇa's claim that all the Ṛgvedic verses were but spells for Vedic *Yajña* is at best a fiction, evidently intended to inflate the veneration for the *yajña* which, from Sāyaṇa's viewpoint, might have served some political purpose.

What is much more interesting for our present discussion is the fact that God—or, for that matter, the Vedic deities—had to suffer their very being in the hands of the later Vedic priesthood, whom Sāyaṇa so much extolled and whose basic philosophical outlook took shape as the Pūrva-mīmāmsā. We shall in our next lecture discuss this philosophy. For the present we have to note another point. The fact remains that considerably later than the *Yajurveda* (and the vast literature called the *Brāhmaṇa*-s, the direct outcome of the Yajurvedic tradition) there emerged a new type of literature, called the Upaniṣads or Vedānta, which were somehow sought to be attached to the Vedic literature. In this there developed a new type of philosophy, inclusive of at least some sort of rudimentary monotheism. What nevertheless is not completely outside the scope of doubt is how far we are entitled to look back at the Upaniṣads as the products of the purely Vedic people. In all likelihood these are the products of a society in which, to repeat the expression of A. Ghose, "the early Aryan society had made room for the Indian society in which it is difficult to isolate Aryan and non-Aryan elements". Indeed, the internal evidences of the Upaniṣads lead us to doubt as to their purely Vedic or Aryan origin, for some of the prominent philosophers in this literature did not clearly have it.

Mahīdāsa Aitareya, from whom the name of the *Aitareya Upaniṣad* is derived, was, on the admission of the orthodox tradition itself, the son of a certain *itarā*, i.e. a low-caste woman according to the Vedic norm, perhaps meaning a woman belonging to the autochthons among whom the Vedic peoples moved and with whom they got intermingled. The story of Jābāla—uncertain of his actual father, his mother having "served" many men—is well-known. It is difficult to believe that Śakaṭavān Raikva—described as scratching his itches while sitting under his cart—could be a sage of pure Vedic origin, because he was a cart-driver rather than a charioteer of the Veda. If there is anything about the Jātaka story of the birth of Uddālaka Āruṇi, namely he owed his name to the Uddalāka tree under which his father united with an autochthon woman, it can hardly be indicative of his pure Vedic origin. Indeed, there are many peculiar names of Upaniṣadic philosophers the roots of which it is hard to trace in the Ṛgvedic tradition.

We have mentioned all this only to emphasise one point. Notwithstanding all that is said about the Upaniṣads as having been the ending portions of the Vedas, the society of which these were the products, like their basic intellectual climate, must have been a new one. Indeed, it was perhaps because of this that when Nārada approached Sanatkumāra with full knowledge of having studied the three Vedas among other subjects, Sanatkumāra bluntly declared that all these were but "mere names" *nāma eva*. A philosopher would have hardly said this about branches of learning *inclusive of the three Vedas* if he were in fact interested in carrying forward the strict Vedic outlook. So also when Śvetaketu returned to his father Uddālaka Āruṇi after having studied the Vedas for a full twelve years, the father, apparently without being impressed by this learning, started asking him philosophical questions unheard of in the Vedas. Incidentally, Śvetaketu—with all his knowledge of the Vedic lore—came to be remembered as the founder of the *Kāma-śāstra*, or the science of erotics rather than the Vedic outlook in any form.

So the evidence of the Upaniṣads—specially of those foreshadowing the monotheistic outlook—proves little or perhaps nothing about the eventual fate of the Vedic gods, though some of them were rather desultorily mentioned in the Upaniṣads. The real custodians of the Vedic tradition—if there were any—were the Vedic priests, whose philosophical view par excellence is to be found in the Pūrvamīmāṁsā. And this Pūrvamīmāṁsā philosophy summarily brushed off the basic concept of God, along with the whole host of the Vedic deities. Such was the eventual fate that the concept of divinity had to suffer at the hands of the most authentic representatives of the Vedic tradition itself.

All this cannot but raise a fundamental question. What exactly is meant by Vedic religion, about which there is so much talk—and so great reverence—in the country? The attempt to seek it in the Upaniṣads has its own problems, some of which we have just mentioned.

Such being the story of it in the Vedic tradition itself, are we then to look for it outside the rigid Vedic literature, i.e. in the beliefs and customs prevalent among the people?

It seems that we are obliged to do it. Here, however, from the strict Vedic viewpoint, perhaps the greatest disappointment awaits us. The great Vedic gods—Indra, Varuṇa, Mitra, Soma—have simply no place in the actual religious beliefs and practices of the vast Indian people. Indra is not totally forgotten, of course. But he is relegated by the Purāṇas to act—though nominally—as the king of gods, indulging mainly in dubious activities. It is evidently difficult—if not impossible—to construct any genuine religious sentiment out of the lusty Purāṇic stories about Indra. Varuṇa, Mitra, Soma and others perhaps suffer a worse fate: they are simply forgotten or perhaps squeezed out of the popular pantheon already overcrowded by all sorts of local deities. In this country of innumerable shrines and temples there is none for the great Vedic gods. As Louis Renou, talking of Varuṇa, observes, "today we have to look to the extreme limit of Indian expansion, the island of Bali, to find a temple dedicated to him".[13] Vedism as religion is simply extinct in India; the Vedic religion has become practically a misnomer. Apart from a few stray sentences or half sentences actually being used in some ritual—which do not really cohere with the rituals as a whole—what in fact survives today in the country is the word *Veda,* and this, specially in the legal literature called the *Dharmaśāstra*-s, mainly as a political instrument to keep the vast masses of the people as law-abiding or loyal citizens. Any law—just or unjust—is loudly proclaimed in the *Dharmaśāstra*-s, to be derived from or sanctioned by the Veda, regardless of course of the circumstance of even any remote vestige of such law actually being found in the Veda—particularly in the *Ṛgveda* which is supposed to have the highest status in the whole range of the Vedic literature. In short, the word Veda became only a political tool rather than the source of any genuine religious sentiment.

REFERENCES

1. L. Woolley in HMCSD I. ii. 458.
2. R.S. Sharma 72.
3. A. Ghosh 2.
4. *Ibid* 4.
5. K. Marx in OR 25.
6. H.P. Sastri HR (Bengali) 389-97.
7. M. Winternitz i. 109.
8. RV i. 122.9, x.85.31; etc.
9. M. Winternitz i. 109.
10. D. Chattopadhyaya L 534 ff.
11. A.A. Macdonell VM 45.
12. *Ibid* 27.
13. L. Renou 44.

5

The Vedic Gods and the Vedic Priests

In my last lecture I have tried to argue that the Vedic religion in its strict sense—i.e. the sense of being the direct outcome of the Vedic literature and as produced by the Vedic people themselves—is really a misnomer. The songs and hymns of the *Ṛgveda* produced by the pastoral nomads and expressing sentiments of the vigorous barbarians, looting food and drinking freely in the company of the deities or *deva*-s, had at best a thin coating of religious sentiment. That is why it could not take roots in the later agricultural communities foreshadowing what the archaeologists call the Second Urbanisation—the beginnings of the historical period. This explains why only from the time of the Upaniṣads—which were the products of a society in which the so-called Aryans were getting freely mixed up with the local people and were adapting their culture, both material and spiritual—things took a somewhat new turn. In the new intellectual climate room was made for the rudiments of religious sentiment in our sense. What is not easily understood, however, is the attitude of the Vedic "priests" themselves, who acquired some sort of abrupt prominence from the time of the *Yajurveda* and the *Brāhmaṇa*-s and claimed to be the exclusive custodians of the Vedic tradition in its strict sense; for the fact is that they preferred to scrap the concept of God altogether and, what appears to us all the more peculiar, proposed virtually to push out of the realm of reality the Vedic deities themselves.

This is so peculiar indeed that before passing on to see how the Vedic priests proposed to scrap the concept of God and virtually pushed out even the Vedic deities from the realm of reality, we may have some idea of the possible motivation of their stark atheism.

For the Vedic priests, the be all and end all is what is called *yajña*. It is usually translated as "sacrifice". Accepting this translation, however, it is necessary to remember that it has absolutely nothing to do with the religious sentiment—with prayer, propitiation, etc.—and hence also with God or any deity. On the contrary, the exclusive assumption on which Vedic *yajña* is based is that the performance of a certain specific act with its appropriate spell automatically—i.e. by the inherent potency of the act itself—ensures the fulfilment of the desires of the rich patrons financing for the sacrifice. In the vast priestly literature, this point is sought to be padded with all sorts of mumbo-jumbo-wild conjectures, weird analogies, absurd etymologies, concocted legends, etc. All this was evidently intended to create a good deal of awe for the *yajña*, obviously required to attract the patrons to pay for it. However, shorn of these mumbo-jumbo-jumbos what we are left with is nothing but the essence of ancient magic.

At the same time, it needs to be remembered that magic, as the characteristic ideology of the primitive pre-class society, had some function and even relevance specially in the context of the collective labour of the primitive society. By contrast, the Vedic *yajña*—though nothing but magic—is transplanted to the sharply class-divided society, which the priestly literature often bluntly eulogises. Thus transplanted, the function of magic passes into its opposite: instead of being an illusory technique supplementing the real technique, it becomes sheer economic drainage, fattening only the parasitical priest-class. Nevertheless, what survives in the Vedic *yajña* is the sense of total redundance of the assumption of God or even the reality of the Vedic deities, which now assumes the form of conscious and stark atheism.

The priestly ideology in its strict sense crystallised in the form of a philosophy which is known as the Pūrva-mīmāṃsā, often referred to simply as Mīmāṃsā. We have to go into some detail of this philosophy to see if it left any scope whatsoever for the religious sentiment.

As a philosophy, the Mīmāṃsā is inconceivable without the Vedas. It intends to thrive on the Vedas, it draws its entire intellectual nourishment from the Vedas, and, in its major part, professes to be nothing more than the right way of understanding the Veda. In fact, the Mīmāṃsā is nothing if not a rationalisation of the Veda. As a rationalisation of the Veda it acquired so much of prestige even in the ancient period that Bādarāyaṇa—the author of the source-book of Vedānta philosophy—with all his distaste for the ontology and epistemology of the Pūrva-mīmāṃsā, felt obliged to show a great deal of respect for Jaimini, who, if not the founḍer of the Mīmāṃsā philosophy, was at least the author of its source-book called the *Mīmāṃsā-sūtra*. Even in the eyes of its opponent, the Vedic orthodoxy of the Mīmāṃsā was absolute.

Nevertheless, the earlier generation of modern scholars felt clearly puzzled by its stark atheism. They wanted to convince themselves that there must have been something wrong somewhere about the professed atheism of the Mīmāṃsā. How could an Indian philosophical view, with an almost fanatical zeal for Vedic orthodoxy, at the same time be so aggressively atheistic?

Max Müller, for example, wonders and suspects some misunderstanding in the traditional view of the Mīmāṃsā attitude to God. Referring to "the charge of atheism that has been brought against Jaimini's Mīmāṃsā", he observes, "This sounds a very strange charge after what we have seen of the character of this philosophy, of its regard for the Veda, and the defence of its revealed character, nay, its insistence on the conscientious observance of all ceremonial injunctions. Still it has been brought both in ancient and in modern times... However, there seems to be a misunderstanding here". He proposes to clear up the misunderstanding with a bold suggestion: "Jaimini would not make the Lord responsible for the injustice that seems to prevail in the world, and hence reduced everything to cause and effect, and saw in the inequities of the world the natural result of the continued action of good or evil acts. This surely was not atheism, rather was it an attempt to clear the Lord from those charges of cruelty or undue partiality which have so often been brought against him.... It was but another attempt at justifying the wisdom of God, an ancient *Theodicee*, that whatever we may think of it, certainly did not deserve the name of atheism... If the Mīmāṃsakas were called atheists, it meant no more than that they tried to justify the ways of God in their own way."[1]

Such a statement, coming as it does from an Indologist of Max Müller's stature, is, to say the least, quite amazing. Far from proving any subtle or veiled defence of theism by Jaimini and his Mīmāṃsā, what it actually proves is that even the eminent modern interpreters of Indian philosophy, when they proceed to discuss the question of God in the Mīmāṃsā, sometimes show little or no interest in the actual Mīmāṃsā literature itself. How far this is due to some preconceived notion of the Vedic view is an interesting question. Into the details of this we cannot unfortunately digress at the moment. Nevertheless, what needs to be emphasised is that there is absolutely no way of reading any bias for theism in the Mīmāṃsā philosophy without resolutely ignoring the Mīmāṃsā literature, or, as Keith puts it rather mildly, "the atheism of the true Mīmāṃsā is regarded with such unanimity as to render it impossible to explain it away".[2]

The Mīmāṃsā literature is quite vast and in it are preserved not only the most determined declarations against the possible existence of God but also bold logical considerations in defence of this declaration. We are to review these in the present and the next lectures. As against Max Müller's statement just quoted, as we shall presently see, Kumārila, one of the greatest representatives of the Mīmāṃsā, far from having any anxiety of saving the almighty God from the charge of creating a world full of evils and inequities, simply laughed at the folly of those that could afford the extravagance to imagine that such a world, full of palpable evils and inequities, could at all be created by an all-powerful and all-merciful God. In other words, the observed evils in this world were for him decisive evidences for the non-existence of God, and, at least as Kumārila thought, no ingenuity of the theist could undermine the importance of these evidences.

But this was not the only evidence for atheism offered by Kumārila nor was Kumārila the only exponent of Mīmāṃsā atheism. All the older and authentic representatives of the Mīmāṃsā view clearly felt that it was necessary for them to deny God in order to make room for the fundamentals of their philosophy, which, in short, is the absolute autonomy of the rituals or yajña. On the other hand, as the right response to it, the authentic representatives of Indian theism felt obliged to argue against the Mīmāṃsā position.

In the *Gītā*, the Lord God himself was made to denounce this philosophy, though mentioning it by name.[3] It remains for us to see, however, that in spite of denunciations like these, the Mīmāṃsakas kept rationalising their atheism most stubbornly.

In the earliest available commentary on the *Mīmāṃsā-sūtra*, Śabara[4] asked, "Have the Vedic gods anything to do with the human lot, or, to be more specific, with ritual actions and their results?" His question was indeed more radical than this, for he wanted to settle even the ontological status of these gods. "Do the Vedic gods", he asked, "have any real or substantive existence?" For a Mīmāṃsaka these questions were of vital importance and Śabara wanted to discuss these with a great deal of earnestness. After satisfying himself that he had reviewed all the considerations on which any substantive being could be attributed to these gods, he came to the conclusion that they could have no existence in the real sense of the term. But, then the fact was that the Vedas mentioned these gods. As mentioned in the Vedas, therefore, what did these gods actually mean? Śabara answered that in the Vedas these stood for mere sounds or words, i.e. the only existence which the Vedic gods had was purely verbal. In his considered judgement, therefore, Agni, Indra, Mitra, Varuṇa, etc. were not divine beings at all. They were mere words instead. Therefore, if there were a hundred synonyms for the word *agni* or fire in the Vedas, these were for Śabara equivalent to a hundred different Vedic deities, the existence of each being constituted by the sound-value of one of the synonyms. It followed from this that, from the Mīmāṃsā point of view, there was no possibility of any interference by these Vedic gods with the human lot. They had nothing to do with the results of human actions. Hence, there was no sense in offering any sacrifice to them. Deprived as they were of any substantive existence, these gods could not accept any offering nor could they feel pleased with these. To try to invoke their grace was thus a senseless act. The rituals produced their result by the inherent potency of their own—rituals in which the names of the gods had value only as forming parts of the spells.

Such then was the mīmāṃsā attitude to God and to the Vedic deities: the former was nothing more than a mere myth and the latter nothing more than mere words. Yet there is no doubt that the Mīmāṃsakas were driven to this attitude by their utmost seriousness for the Vedas.

In other words, their rejection of both monotheism and polytheism followed from their adherence to the Vedas, or, to be more precise, from the way in which they themselves understood the Vedas.

To the average Indian today, all these may appear to be strange and even bewildering. It will, however, be hasty to think that the real reason for this is that the Mīmāṃsakas thoroughly misunderstood the Vedas. On the contrary, they themselves lived in the Vedic tradition and were too involved in it to misunderstand it. There was an almost unbroken continuity between at least one aspect of the Vedic tradition and the Mīmāṃsā philosophy, the latter being both historically and logically only a culmination of the former.

If, therefore, we fail to understand today how an almost fanatical zeal for the Vedas led the Mīmāṃsakas to accept a radical form of atheism, the real reason for this is likely to be that the enormous time-gap between the Vedas and ourselves has resulted for us in the loss of some vital aspect of the ancient Vedic tradition. This means, in short, that our view of the Vedic view is in need of serious revision.

We shall return later to discuss all this more fully. For the present, we may note that even some of the later representatives of the Mīmāṃsā system felt puzzled by the stark atheism of the philosophy they were themselves expounding. One of the best known examples of this was Khaṇḍadeva, a Mīmāṁsaka of the seventeenth century. After explaining the fundamentals of the Mīmāṁsā, he stood aghast as it were by what he had himself written. While trying to be faithful to the spirit of Jaimini, he found it impossible to allow even a scrap of theism in the philosophy he expounded. At the same time, evidently because of being personally cut off from something vital in the ancient Vedic tradition and perhaps also because of the strong authority of the Indian law-makers boosting the Vedānta philosophy in his own time—he clearly felt that the categorical stand against God inevitably embodied in his exposition of the Mīmāṃsā, must have been a sin or a sacrilege. He wanted, therefore, to atone for this sin and concluded his treatise with a strange prayer. "Thus", he said, "are explained the essence of Jaimini's views. Even by the mere utterance of these, my words have become polluted. So my only refuge consists in invoking the grace of God."[5]

This is how, under the changed atmosphere of the later days, a genuine Mīmāṃsaka looked back at the Mīmāṃsā atheism. Others, obviously with lesser scruple for the original spirit of the philosophy, wanted somehow or other to convert it into a theistic one. Understandably enough, the development of such a tendency among the Mīmāṃsakas themselves helps Radhakrishnan to feel somewhat relieved after all. Referring to the absence of God in the Mīmāṃsā philosophy, he comments, "This lacuna of the Pūrva-mīmāṃsā was so unsatisfactory that the later writers slowly *smuggled in God*".[6] He mentions in this connection the examples of Vedānta Deśika and Āpadeva. Of these two, the former produced a strange work called the *Seśvara-mīmāṃsā* or "Mīmāṃsā with God", while the latter advanced the thesis—also strange from the Mīmāṃsā point of view—that during the time of the universal dissolution (*pralaya*), the Vedas remained in the memory of God. What Radhakrishnan does not add, however, is that the mention of Vedānta Deśika in the context of the true Mīmāṃsā is irrelevant after all, it being well known that his real philosophical affiliation was to the Rāmānuja version of the Vedānta, which was most theistic of all the forms of Vedānta. In other words, he was perhaps trying to smuggle the Mīmāṃsā ideas into the framework of his own theism rather than trying to smuggle in God into the Mīmāṃsā philosophy. Besides, as it is rightly observed, the very title of his work, namely "Mīmāṃsā with God", shows how little the real Mīmāṃsā had to do with God. Similarly, Āpadeva's theory that God retained the Vedas during the time of *pralaya*, could be advanced only in complete disregard of the older and authentic standpoint of the Mīmāṃsā philosophy, according to which the very conception of *pralaya*, like that of *sṛṣṭi* or creation, was only a figment of the theist's imagination. Thus, in short, the later tendencies of reconciling the Mīmāṃsā philosophy with the view of god or the gods amounted only to the upsetting of the fundamentals of this philosophy.

With these introductory words, we may now pass on to discuss Mīmāṃsā atheism in some detail.

This is perhaps best done in two steps.

First, by reviewing the earliest Mīmāṃsā literature available for us. Secondly, by reviewing the works of the later philosophers of the Mīmāṃsā school when they were obliged to face the monotheistic arguments developed by their rivals.

We have proposed these two steps, because there is some substantial difference between the two.

The early Mīmāṃsā literature gives us the impression that it was the product of a period when monotheistic ideas were yet to take full shape. What the early Mīmāṃsakas were concerned with was mainly the question of the Vedic deities, or, more specifically, with the question of such deities having any substantive existence. In the history of Indian philosophy, however, in a much later period took shape distinctly monotheistic ideas—first among a section of the followers of the Vedānta and then among the later Nyāya-Vaiśeṣikas. The Mīmāṃsakas of later days could not ignore or bypass these ideas. They had to settle the account of the Mīmāṃsā position with later theism.

The earliest available Mīmāṃsā work is the *Mīmāṃsā-sūtra* attributed to a certain Jaimini. For understanding it, we are obliged to depend on Śabara's commentary on it.

The question that interested them vitally was: How were we to understand the exact nature of the Vedic *yajña*-s in relation to the Vedic *deva*-s, i.e. the Vedic rituals in relations to the Vedic gods? Were the gods primary and the ritual secondary, so that the rituals were nothing but acts of worshipping the gods? As a matter of fact, argued the Mīmāṃsakas, the actual relation between the two was just the reverse. The rituals were primary and the gods not even secondary but mere words useful for the rituals. The Mīmāṃsakas discussed the question threadbare and came to the conclusion that the actual status of the gods was that of mere words, i.e. in modern terminology, of mere sounds forming parts of the ritual spell.

The main discussion of the nature of the Vedic gods is to be found in the Mīmāṃsā-sūtra ix. 1.6-10 and Śabara's commentary on these. Following primarily Nilakantha Sastry's admirable translation[7] of these, let us first review the main arguments of the Mīmāṃsakas intended to prove that the rituals were primary compared to the gods and that the actual status of the Vedic gods was after all nominal. This discussion is in two parts. First, the *pūrvapakṣa* or the statement of the position of the opponent. Secondly, the *siddhānta* or the refutation of the opponent and the conclusion of the Mīmāṃsakas themselves. In my book *Indian Atheism*, I have quoted the entire discussion of all this. Nevertheless, in view of the importance of it for understanding the problem of Vedic religion being a myth or reality, I cannot help reiterating it here over again.

The View of the Opponent

The case of a theistic understanding of the Vedic gods:

The deity, it is claimed, is primary and the *yajña* is for the sake of the deity. The *yajña* is in fact a form of worshipping the deity. The deity causes the *yajña* to be performed. And the food offered in the *yajña* is for the sake of the deity, just as food offered to the guest.

It is wrong to imagine that Agni and others are not the inducing agents of the *yajña*. On the contrary, the deities are the instigators of the sacred acts. Why? Because the meal offered in the *yajña* is for the sake of the deity. What is known as the ritual is nothing but the offering of food to the deities. This is evident from the fact that edible things are offered to the deity, with the statement that the deity shall eat these.

Further, the name of the deity is mentioned in the ritual in the dative case and, compared to the accusative case, the use of the dative case is indicative of something more directly aimed at. Therefore, the deity is not secondary. On the contrary, the materials used in that ritual act itself are secondary with reference to the deity.

Thus, the ritual is only an act of worshipping the deity. Compared to the object of worship, the act of worshipping is always observed to be secondary. Just as in the case of the guest any entertainment is for the sake of pleasing him, so must be the ritual performed for the sake of pleasing the deity.

It may be objected that the acceptance of all these amounts to the admission of the deity having a human form for actually eating the offerings. To this objection it is replied that the deity does have a form and the deity does eat. But what is the proof of all these? The theist argues that all these are proved by Tradition (*smṛti*), Popular Belief (*upacāra*) and Circumstantial Evidence *(anyārthadarśana)*.

Thus, according to tradition—which is a valid evidence—the deity does possess a form. And people believe the same to be true. Hence they paint Yama with a rod in his hands, Varuṇa with a noose and Indra with a thunderbolt. In this way, the popular belief strengthens the evidence of tradition. And circumstantial evidence also converges on the same point. Thus, for example, it is said in the *Ṛgveda:* "Oh, Indra, thy right arm we caught." This shows that Indra must have a human form, because the right arm and left arm are characteristic of the human form. If Indra is imagined to have no form, the statement of the *Ṛgveda* makes no sense. Similarly, in the *Ṛgveda* is said: "These two, heaven and earth, that are far apart, thou graspest, Oh Maghavan, thy fist is great." This also makes sense only if the deity is assumed to have human form. Again, the *Ṛgveda* says, "Indra, transported with juice of Soma, vast in his belly, strong in his neck and with stout arms smites Vṛtra down." This also presupposes that Indra has a belly, a neck and arms, which are indicative of human form alone. From all these it is clear that the Vedic gods possess human form.

But how is it claimed that the gods also eat? From tradition, popular belief and circumstantial evidence, again. Thus tradition or *smṛti* declares that the deity eats. People also believe that the deity eats, otherwise there can be no sense in their bringing all sorts of food for the deities and offering these to the deities. From circumstantial evidence also we have to infer that the deity eats. Thus, for example, are said in the *Ṛgveda*: "Eat Indra, and drink of that which stirs to meet thee." "All kinds of food within his maw he gathers." "(Indra) at a single draught drank the contents of thirty pails." All these make sense only on the admission that the gods actually eat.

It may be objected that if the gods actually eat, the food offered to them should diminish in quantity. But the foods offered to the gods are not observed to diminish in quantity.

To this it is replied that the deities actually eat the essence of the food offered to them, just as the bees take only the honey from the flower. In spite of the honey being taken from the flower by the bees, the flower is not observed to suffer any quantitative loss. So is the food offered to the deity. Nevertheless, just as the flower becomes honeyless, so does the food; the food becomes tasteless after it is offered to the gods. This proves that the gods eat the essence of the food offered to them.

Further, the worship of the gods in order to propitiate them becomes meaningful only if they are assumed to be the lords of the material objects which they bestow as favour on being entertained. In other words, the worship of the deity can have a meaning only if the deity is assumed to be lord of the material objects. Hence the theist proposes to prove that the deities are actual lords of the material objects. But how to prove this? The theist claims that this is proved by tradition, popular belief and circumstantial evidence. Tradition clearly declares that the deities are the masters of all the good things of life. This is corroborated by popular belief. Thus, people speak of "the deity's village," "the deity's field" and so on. Circumstantial evidence also indicates the actual lordship of the deity. Thus, for example, the *Ṛgveda* says: "Indra is sovereign lord of heaven and earth. Indra is lord of waters and of clouds. Indra is lord of prosperers and sages. Indra must be invoked in rest and efforts." Again: "Looker-on of everything, lord of this moving world, lord, Indra, of what moveth not." And so on. Evidently, these passages cannot make any sense if the deity is not considered the actual lord of the things.

Further, from tradition, popular belief and circumstantial evidences it is also clear that the deity does bestow favours. Tradition or *smṛti* declares this in so many words. Besides, there are expressions of the popular belief in the form: "Prajāpati is pleased with him; hence a son is born of him." "Vaiśravaṇa is pleased with him; hence he has obtained wealth." Circumstantial evidence concurs. Thus, for example, it is declared in the *Ṛgveda*: "It is as if one pleases the gods who are offering-eaters—by means of fire-offerings, etc. Gods in their pleasure give one food and sap of food." How can a passage like this make sense if we do not admit that the deity does bestow favours?

From all these it is only reasonable to conclude that the connection between the ritual acts and their results is effected by the gods. The deity connects the worshipper with the fruit of worship. Whoever approaches the deity with offerings, him the deity connects with the fruits of his deeds. The proofs of this, again, consist of tradition, popular belief and circumstantial evidence. Tradition declares that the deity favours him who sacrifices. This evidence of tradition is strengthened by popular belief. Thus, for example, according to the popular belief one obtains a son by worshipping Paśupati. Further, circumstantial evidence concurs. Thus, e.g., in the *Ṛgveda* is said: "He with his folk, his house, his family, his sons, gains booty for himself, and with the heroes, wealth, who, with oblation and a true believing heart serves Brahmaṇaspati, the father of the gods." Again, the *Ṛgveda* says, "Only when satisfied himself, does Indra satisfy this person with offering and cattle."

From all these it is clear that by offering food and prayers, the god is worshipped; being worshipped thus he is pleased; being pleased he offers the fruits or results of the worship. Agni, for example, is the lord of something particular; being worshipped in a particular form, he bestows the particular thing to the worshipper. Another god—Sūrya for example—cannot bestow the same thing. From the Vedas we learn which god can give what. Accordingly, something is said in the Vedas of Agni and not Sūrya, i.e. something else of Sūrya.

Answer to the Opponent

Refutation of the theistic understanding of the Vedic gods:

Verbal testimony (Veda) proves that the *yajña* should be held as primary and the mention of the deity secondary.

It is not correct to claim that the gods are inducing agents.

What is supremely important is the ritual act itself. The performance of the ritual act generates *apūrva*. [This being one of the basic ideas of the Mīmāṃsakas it may be explained here. Apūrva literally means "not existing before." Technically, however, it is taken by the Mīmāṃsakas to mean "the resultant of any action (*karma*) in an invisible stage which it is supposed to assume before producing visible results." Thus, the act is supposed to lead to some result, though the result is not observed to take place immediately after the performance of the act. Nevertheless, there is no discontinuity between the act and the result: during the interval between the act and its result, the *apūrva*, directly resulting from the act, remains operative in an invisible form and this *apūrva* ultimately leads to the final result].

As against the theistic understanding of the Yajña, therefore, the Mīmāṃsakas argue that its performance directly generates the *apūrva* and this *apūrva* ultimately leads to the result designed. But how is it proved that the performance of the ritual directly generates the *apūrva*? Śabara answers that this is proved by verbal testimony, i.e. specifically the Vedas. In fact, in these matters the only relevant proof is the evidence of verbal testimony or Vedas. "The knowledge that any thing gives fruits, i.e. any inducing agent gives a particular fruit, arises from verbal testimony and not from direct perception or any other source of knowledge." And, according to verbal testimony or the Vedas, the fruit is derived from the *yajña* itself and not from the *deva*-s. Thus, the Vedas declare: "He who desires heaven (incidentally, 'heaven' in the Mīmāṃsā philosophy means simply 'pleasure' not necessarily other-worldly) should perform the Darśa and Pūrṇamāsa rituals." "He who desires heaven (pleasure) should perform the Jyotiṣṭoma ritual." Thus, in the context of the desire for heaven or pleasure, what is mentioned is the *yajña* and not the *deva*. However, are not the ritual materials *(dravya)* and the deities *(deva)* also mentioned in connection with the *yajña*? That is true. However, the mention of the deity is secondary. The requisite materials and the gods are supposed to be already there, whereas the ritual is something yet to be performed. When something already existing is mentioned along with something that has to be brought into existence, the existent is mentioned for the sake of the non-existent. Therefore, the gods are not the inducing agents.

As against the claim of the opponent that the deity is directly aimed at by the use of the dative termination, Śabara argues that from the same source, namely the Vedas, it is clearly seen that the ritual act itself is directly connected with the designed result. The Vedas speak of the instrumentality of the *yajña* itself and not of the *deva* in producing the fruit. This fruit or result is the real *puruṣārtha* or that which is the aim of man and the endeavour for the sake of the *puruṣārtha* is ours and not that of the deity. Therefore, we do not perform any action on account of the inducement from the gods. And the mention of the deity's name with the dative ending easily agrees with the idea that the deity is the means to the performance of the fruitful *yajña*.

The opponent claims: "*Yajña* is worship of the deity and the object of worship is the primary thing in worship, as we see it in the world." To this Śabara answers that such a view of the *yajña* is untenable. That which is fruitful is the inducing agent and the inducing agent is the ritual itself.

In defence of the position of the opponent, namely that the *yajña* is nothing but an act of worship, the opponent has to admit that the deity has a form and that it actually eats, because there can be no gift or meal for a deity which is without any form and which it does not eat. In defence of his view, the opponent cites the proofs of tradition, popular belief and circumstantial evidences. Śabara, therefore, refutes, these proofs of the deity having a form and as actually eating.

Tradition or *smṛti,* argues Śabara, cannot prove that the deity has a form and that it eats. *Smṛti* is based on the *mantra*-s and *artha-vāda*-s: it is a matter of direct perception that all knowledge on which tradition rests is derived from these. And, we shall presently see (Śabara, on the *Mīmāṃsā-*

sūtra x. 4.23), that the *mantra*-s and *arthavāda*-s do not at all support such a view of the deities. It is useless, argues Śabara, to try to deny that the real basis of tradition is *mantra* and *arthavāda*. Only a superficial view of *smṛti* may lead one to imagine that it is independent of *mantra* and *arthavāda*. As for popular belief, Śabara argues that it can be valid only in so far as it is based on tradition or *smṛti* itself.

Thus, popular belief cannot prove that the gods have form and that they actually eat the offerings.

Śabara next takes up the question of the circumstantial evidence *(anyārthadarśana)* proving that the Vedic gods actually possess human form. The argument, in short, is simple. Without admitting the human form, a large number of Vedic passages make no sense at all. Thus, for example, the Ṛgveda declares, "Oh Indra thy right arm we caught." Does this not clearly imply that Indra does possess a right arm and, therefore, also the human form? If the Vedas are full of declarations like these, how can the Mīmāṃsakas profess fidelity to the Vedic authority and at the same time deny that the gods possess human forms?

Śabara answers that it is impossible to take these Vedic passages in these apparent or superficial senses. Thus, for example, the apparent meaning of the passages of the *Ṛgveda* is that we hold the right arm of Indra. However, does the *Ṛgveda* really mean this? The answer must be in the negative, for it is a matter of direct perception that we do not hold the right arm of Indra. These Vedic passages, therefore, lead us to face two clear-cut alternatives. Either, taking these in their apparent or superficial sense, we have to admit that what the *Ṛgveda* refers to is just an absurdity; or, we have to reject this apparent sense and accept the passages in some other deeper sense. The first of these alternatives is clearly untenable. If the Vedas refer to certain absurdities, what is the use of citing their authority? Since, therefore, the Vedas cannot contain absurdities, the apparent meaning of these passages which suggest these absurdities must be rejected. Thus, in short, the real meaning of the Vedic passages like these must be something else. What, then is this real meaning? The answer of Śabara is not difficult to see. The real implication of the passages like these must be mere praise—*stuti* or *arthavāda*. By this the Mīmāṃsakas mean some form of indirect glorification of certain ritual actions. Thus, for example, the real meaning of the passage of the *Ṛgveda* under consideration is the indirect glorification of the *yajña* or ritual in which something is referred to as the right arm of Indra and not that Indra really possesses a right arm.

As against this, the opponent may claim that the Vedic passage under consideration may be taken as the statement of a man who in the past held Indra's arm. That is, by direct perception the fact of somebody holding Indra's arm cannot be proved, because such an event does not take place at the present time. Nevertheless, it is quite conceivable that in the past somebody actually held Indra's arm and the Vedic passage under consideration is a mere record of this experience as stated by him.

Such a line of argument is rejected outright by Śabara, inasmuch as it goes directly against the fundamental Mīmāṃsā thesis that the Vedas are eternal and absolutely impersonal *(apauruṣeya)*. As a matter of fact, it is one of the fundamental theses of the Mīmāṃsā philosophy and the Mīmāṃsakas themselves are fully satisfied that they have proved it beyond any possible scope for doubt. Therefore, there can be no question from the Mīmāṃsā point of view of the possibility of the Vedas retaining any statement of anybody. In short, there is no other way but to accept the Vedic passage as an *arthavāda,* i.e. the glorification of a ritual action with the mention of Indra *(indrakarma)*. It remains for us to see what, from the Mīmāṃsā point of view, can be the real implication of the mention of a deity like Indra in a ritual act.

The opponent may argue that there is no sense in praising what does not exist. If Indra has no arm at all, it is meaningless even as praise to speak of Indra's arm. Śabara answers that the objection is not valid, for even if a thing is not necessarily connected with (i.e. does not possess) human attributes, it is sometimes praised as if it had human attributes. Thus, for example, a hymn of the *Ṛgveda* has for its deity "the stones" and in this the stones are praised as follows: "They speak out like a hundred, like a thousand men; they cry aloud to us with their green-tinted mouth. During the *yajña,* these pious stones taste the offered food even before Agni." Similarly, another hymn has for its deity "the rivers" and in this the river is praised as follows: "Sindhu hath yoked her car, light rolling, drawn by steed". In these passages, things having no likeness to human form at all, are praised as if these possessed the human form. Therefore, from the Vedic passages, there can be no presumption (*arthāpatti*) of the human likeness of the Vedic gods. Even if the human form of a deity is apparently mentioned, we cannot conclude that the passage cannot be understood without assuming that the deity does possess a human form.

The expression "broad-necked Indra" in the Veda does not mean that Indra possesses a neck. What can it mean then? It simply means the glorification of something which is simply referred to as the neck of Indra, though this something is not actually the neck of Indra.

In this way, after elaborately reviewing the Vedic passages alleged to refer to the Vedic gods as possessing human form, Śabara comes to the conclusion, "Therefore, there is no circumstantial evidence that indicates that the deity has human likeness."

Following Jaimini, he next proceeds to prove that the *yajña* is not a meal, the deity does not eat and, therefore, the claim that the deity is more important than the *yajña* because the meal is for the deity's sake, is absolutely untenable. The possibility of the deity actually eating the food offered to it is already disproved, of course, by the proof of the deity having no human form. Nevertheless, since Śabara offers in this connection a number of delightfully commonsense considerations against the popular belief of the theist, we may quote him at some length.

"As for the statement that from tradition, popular belief and circumstantial evidence we learn that the deity eats—this has already been refuted by proving that the deity has no human form." In other words, the possibility of eating presupposes the possession of a body and since the deity cannot have a body it is idle to imagine that it is capable of eating. "Further", adds Śabara, "the meal offered to a deity who actually eats should diminish in quantity. And there is no proof that the deities eat the essence of the food in the manner of the bee. There is direct perception in the case of the bee and it is not there in the case of the deity. Therefore, the deity does not eat. The statement that the meal offered to the deity becomes tasteless creates no difficulty. The food becomes tasteless and cold on account of the exposure to the air."

The theists claim that the *yajña* is a form of worship by which the deity is pleased and the deity eventually bestows the results. Such a claim rests on the assumption that the deity is actually the lord of the material goods: how can the deity give us the goods without himself possessing these or being the lord of these? However, argues Śabara, the assumption that the deity is the lord of the material goods is totally untenable.

"It cannot be claimed that from tradition, popular belief and circumstantial evidence we can infer the lordship of the deity." Tradition is based on the Vedic injunctions and the 'praise of the injunctions' *(arthavāda)* and there is nothing in the Vedic injunctions and their praises to indicate that the deity is actually the lord of things. Popular belief in the form "the deity's village," "the deity's field", etc. are mere beliefs without any real basis. Only that can be considered as one's property which one can dispose of at one's mere will. The deity, however, cannot at his mere will dispose of the village or the land. Therefore, the gods do not give anything. "And for the statement that circumstantial evidence shows the lordship of the deity—as in 'Indra is the lord of heaven', etc.—

knowing by direct perception that the deity has no lordship, we infer that these words are figurative."

It may be objected that from the Vedas we learn the lordship of the deity. Thus, for example, it is said in the Vedas that the gods distribute all good things and from this we infer that this is only because the gods will it, i.e. the will of the gods is the real cause of the distribution of all good things. To this Śabara replies that such an understanding of the verbal testimony of the Vedas must evidently be wrong. From direct perception we know that the real cause of obtaining all good things is the will of the performer of the act or of the *yajña,* which mentions the deity. This will of the performer of the act can never be secondary. Even those who describe the deity as omnipotent cannot overlook the part of the will of the performer of the act. Therefore, they say that the deity bestows the good things according to the act of the performer of the *yajña*. However, since the gods cannot bestow things according to their own will and have to follow instead the will of others, how can they be conceived as the real lords? Further, the alleged verbal testimony or the evidence of the Vedas is really not there. That is, the Vedas do not actually declare that the gods distribute all good things. On account of the statement quoted being opposed by direct perception, the only sense in which the statement can be taken is some praise of the *yajña* enjoined in the Vedas. When such expressions could be (easily) explained as intended for praise (of the ritual injunction itself), these cannot be taken as verbal testimony proving the lordship of the deity. And the deity can never connect the man with the fruit of his act.

Such then, was the attitude to the Vedic deities in the early Mīmāṃsā literature. In my next lecture I shall try to discuss the reaction of the later Mīmāṃsakas, to the monotheistic ideas, particularly of Kumārila, whom a scholar as eminent as Satkari Mukherjee considers to be the greatest of the traditional Indian philosophers.

REFERENCES

1. F. Max Müller CW. xix. 210.
2. A.B. Keith KM 60.
3. *Gītā* ii.42-44.
4. *Śabara* on MS i. 1.5.
5. *Khaṇḍadeva, Bhātta-dīpikā iii. 53.*
6. S. Radhakrishnan IP. ii. 427.
7. N. Sastry in. IA Vol. 50, 211 ff. & 240 ff.

6

God and the Later Mīmāṃsakas

According to the view which Kumārila[1] rejected first, God was the exclusive or sole-sufficient cause of everything or the creator of everything. As against such an absolute view of the creator, Kumārila began with a number of simple commonsense considerations.

The upholder of such a view must admit that God existed before the creation of anything whatsoever, i.e. he must admit that before the act of creation God and God alone existed. However, if nothing else existed at that time—no space, no universe, nothing—wherein could the creator himself conceivably stay and how can we at all know that he did exist at such a time? "At a time when all this did not exist, what could have been the condition of the universe? As for the creator (Prajāpati) himself, what could be his position? and what his form? And at that time (when none else existed), who would know him and explain his character to the later created persons? Without the perception (or knowledge in some form of God at a time before the creation) how can we at all assume (the fact of his existence at that time)?" In other words, the theist cannot in any way prove the existence of the creator before the act of creation, nor has he any satisfactory answer to the question concerning the position of God before the creation of the universe, because on his own admission nothing but God existed before creation.

Further, the theist will have to admit that this creator either possesses a body or that he does not. Both these alternatives, however are untenable. If God is viewed as being without a body, he cannot have any desire whatsoever—not even the desire for creation—and he cannot create without any desire to create. If, to avoid this difficulty, the theist admits that god does possess a body, he will have to face all sorts of troublesome questions to which there are no satisfactory answers. "Then, again," argued Kumārila, "in what manner do you believe the world to have had a beginning in time? (If it be held that it is brought about by a desire on the part of the creator), since the creator is without a material body, etc. how could He at all have any desire to create? And, if He has a body, assuredly this body would not have been created by Himself. Thus, then, we would have to postulate another creator (for His body; and so on *ad infinitum*). If the creator's body is held to be eternal (we ask) —so long as earth, etc. have not been produced, of what material would that body be composed?"

But the question of the body apart, the very assumption of any desire on the part of the creator to create our world is untenable, for the world is full of evils and why should God at all want to create an evil world? "Then, again, in the first place, how is it that He should have a desire to create a world which is to be fraught with all sorts of troubles to living beings? For at that time (i.e. at the beginning of creation), He has not got any guiding agencies in the shape of virtue (and sin), etc. of the living beings themselves. Nor can any creator create anything in the absence of any means and instruments." As the commentators explained, "People hold that all the troubles in this world are due to the vicious deeds of the living beings in their previous births. This may be quite true. However, at the beginning of creation, there being no previous birth of anybody, no such guiding principle would be available and the blame of creating a troublesome world would rest only on God himself."

More of this problem of evil later. For the present Kumārila argued that even granting the agency of virtue and vice, that alone could not have sufficed for the creation of the world. For producing something, it was necessary to have the required materials for production. The potter, for example, produced the jar, because he had the required materials in the form of clay, etc. But the creator, according to the theist, had no such material and hence it was not possible for him to create. In answer to such an objection, the stock example cited by the theist was that of the spider which spun the cobweb from out of itself, i.e. without the need of any external material required for production. And, if the spider could create something without being provided with any external material for production, it was useless to think that God was incapable of doing it. As against, this, Kumārila argued that the theist thoroughly misunderstood the example of the spider.

As a matter of fact, the spider did not produce anything from out of nothing or exclusively from itself. On the contrary, it produced the cobweb from some definite external material. In the words of Kumārila, "Even the production of the spider's web is not to be viewed as being without any material basis: the web is produced by the saliva which, in its turn is produced from the bodies of the insects eaten by the spider."

Kumārila next took up the question of the possible motive that could have led God to create the world. The usual answer of the theist to this question was that God was motivated to create the world by compassion or pity for the living beings. Such an answer, argued Kumārila, was useless. (If it is argued that God created the world out of compassion for the living beings, we reply:) In the absence of the objects of compassion (i.e. the living beings), no compassion could be possible for him. And, if he moved to create by pure compassion, he should have created only happy beings."

As against the second of these arguments, the typical defence of the theist is the theory of necessary evil: some amount of pain or evil was indispensable for the creation of the world, just as for making a golden ornament a certain amount of alloy is necessary to be mixed with gold. Kumārila replied that such a defence of theism was completely unsatisfactory. The theist himself claimed that God was omnipotent. Nothing, therefore, could impose a limit to his activity. Hence the view that some amount of evil was indispensable for creation could not be binding on him. Or, if it was really binding on him, the theist had no right to claim that God was actually omnipotent. "If it be argued", said Kumārila, "that without some pain neither creation nor the continuation of the world would be possible, (we reply:) When everything depends on the mere will of the creator himself, what could be impossible for him? And if he were to depend upon laws and agencies, this fact would deprive him of his (boasted) independence."

The alleged act of creation, continued Kumārila, must have been either without any definite purpose or with some definite purpose. If it was without any purpose, the act must have been utterly foolish and hence the alleged intelligence of God was only a fiction. If, on the other hand, it was with some definite purpose, this very purpose must have been indicative of some want in God, which could not be fulfilled without creation. In this alternative, therefore, the theist had to surrender his claim that God was all-perfect. "What is the end", asked Kumārila, "which he desires and which could not be gained without creating the world? Without some end in view, even a fool does not act. If he were to act so (i.e. without any end in view), what would be the good of his intelligence?"

To this the famous answer of Bādarāyaṇa, the Vedāntist was that the creation of the world by God was to be viewed as some kind of sport or play (*līlā*). The kings engage themselves in the act of hunting not because they want to satisfy thereby any specific want, but because it is a mere pastime for them. So are the children found to play for having the sheer fun of the game. Similarly, God's creation of the world is to be viewed as a sport or a pastime, rather than as an act designed to satisfy some definite want. This, argued Kumārila, led the theists to contradict themselves. "If the activity of the creator were due to a desire for mere amusement, that would go against his ever-contentedness. And (instead of affording any amusement), the great amount of work (required for creation) would be a source of infinite trouble for him. And his desire to destroy the world (at the time of *pralaya* or periodic cosmic dissolution), assumed by the theist would be hardly explicable."

A number of internal contradictions were thus involved in the position of the theist. However, these contradictions apart, the very assumption of the theist that there was a God who created the world, was, in Kumārila's view, beyond the scope of any possible evidence. He argued this in an apparently light mood and wanted to make fun of the theist's position.

"And such a creator could never be known by anybody. Even if he were known in form, the fact of his being the creator could never be known. Because, at that time (i.e. the time of creation), what could the living beings, appearing at the beginning of creation, understand? They could not understand wherefrom they have been born; nor could they know the state of the world prior to creation, nor the fact of God being the creator. Nor could the idea that they would derive from his own assertion—which is generally considered as scriptural evidence or evidence derived from direct revelation—with regard to his being the creator) be altogether trustworthy; because even though he may not have created the world, he might have spoken of having done so, in order to show off his great power."

For the theists—particularly for the followers of the Vedānta or the Upaniṣads—the main proof for the existence of God and of the creation of the world by him consisted of scriptural declarations. The plain meaning of many passages of the Vedas suggests that God is the creator of the universe. It was possible for the Buddhist or Jain philosophers to ignore the evidence of these passages altogether. But this could not be so for Kumārila. To the Mīmāṃsakas the validity of the Vedas was absolute. How, then, were they to stick to their atheism in spite of the Vedic passages declaring in favour of

God having been the creator, or, for that matter, of theism in general?

The question is interesting and it leads us to see the skill of the Mīmāṃsakas in contriving the principles of textual interpretation. They argued, in short, that the apparent meaning of these Vedic passages could not be their real meaning. The real meaning of all the Vedic passages was somehow or other connected with the injunctions concerning the Vedic rituals. Any passage which was not apparently so—and which was apparently descriptive instead of being imperative—was to be interpreted as being a round-about or indirect praise of some injunction, i.e. as having for its real theme the injunction itself. In Mīmāṃsā terminology, this was called *arthavāda,* which roughly meant the technique of interpreting those passages of the Vedas that had apparently no connection with the ritual injunctions in a way as to mean the indirect praise of ritual injunctions.

How far the Mīmāṃsākas actually succeeded in interpreting all the Vedic passages in this way is a different question altogether. For the present the point rather is that they refused to admit God even on scriptural evidences. Those passages of the Vedas that apparently mentioned God and described him as creating the world could prove the position of the theist only if grossly misunderstood. On the contrary, the actual implication of these passages was some indirect praise of the ritual injunctions and this implication became clear if the passages were understood in their proper context.

Therefore, Kumārila argued that the Vedic passages apparently referring to God and His creation were not to be taken as actual evidences for the existence of God. As he put it, "The idea common among ordinary people (that the Veda mentions creation as proceeding from Prajāpati) is a mistaken one, caused by certain eulogies *(stutivākya:* passages praising injunctions), because when a passage is not duly considered and interpreted together with the passages that precede and follow it, it is bound to give rise to a misconception."

Similar, argued Kumārila, was the real implication of certain passages of the *Mahābhārata* and the Purāṇas which, only as superficially understood or basically misunderstood, could be taken as referring to God and his creation. Incidentally, for the Vedāntic theists the strongest proofs for the existence of God were the scriptural or Vedic declarations in favour of him. Vedānta as a philosophy had little confidence in independent reasoning arriving at right conclusions concerning the ultimate reality and therefore intended only to be a systematisation of the real implication of the Vedic—particularly the Upaniṣadic—passages. Hence the claim of Kumārila that no Vedic passage actually proved the existence of God amounted to summarily ignoring the strongest proof of God which the Vedāntists were aware of. Incidentally, from the Mīmāṃsā viewpoint, the entire Upaniṣadic literature was to be considered as *arthavāda*—i.e. instead of being understood as what it plainly meant was rather to be understood as some way of glorifying the *yajña*!

Refuting thus the doctrine of God which was perhaps originally advanced by Bādarāyaṇa in his *Bhrama-sūtra*, Kumārila proceeded to the critical rejection of the view of God as advanced by the later Nyāya-Vaiśeṣikas. He began this discussion by pointing to certain internal inconsistencies of the Nyāya-Vaiśeṣika theology, that evidently developed in some later period.

Thus, for example, he argued that the Nyāya-Vaiśeṣika conception of *pralaya* or universal dissolution—like its theological counterpart namely the conception of creation—hardly made any sense. Further, though the Nyāya-Vaiśeṣika conceived God merely as the efficient cause of the world—and were thus comparatively free from the difficulties of the other theists who conceived God as creating the world without being provided with any material necessary for the purpose—yet they were by no means free from the difficulties of pointing to any possible motive that might have led God to create the world. The theological inconsistencies like these, which, according to Kumārila, were involved in the theism of the Nyāya-Vaiśeṣikas, do not appear to have major philosophical interest for us. We may, therefore, quote here only a brief summary of this aspect of Kumārila's criticism of the Nyāya-Vaiśeṣika position: "Against the Vaiśeṣika view of creation, exception is justly taken to the difficulty involved in holding that in some manner the action of the Supreme Lord brings to a stand at one time (i.e. at the time of *pralaya)* the potencies of all the souls, and then awakens them all when a new creation is imminent. Against this view it is contended that the activity of men arising from their past deeds can never cease, and it is absurd and needless to complicate matters by assuming both the force of men's deeds and the intervention of the desire of God. Moreover, it is impossible to explain why this desire should ever arise and it is unintelligible to think of any mode in which the creator can act without a body or acquire a body."

After explaining the nature of the theological inconsistencies like these, Kumārila took up for critical examination the Nyāya-Vaiśeṣika inference of God, according to which anything made of parts must presuppose an intelligent maker thereof and since everything in the world is made of parts (atoms), the totality of the things in nature must point to a supreme intelligent maker, viz. God. "As against those," said Kumārila, "who argue that the production of the body, etc. must presuppose the superintendence or control of an intelligent agent, because these are made of constituent parts, as for instance the house, etc.—our answer is as follows." And he proceeded to explain the number of fallacies involved in this inference.

First, what exactly is meant by this superintendence or control of an intelligent agent? Is it to be understood in its most general sense?

In that case, it can mean nothing more than the superintendence or control of an intelligent agent in some form or other without specifying the nature of this intelligent agent. In other words, is the Nyāya-Vaiśeṣika inference intended only to prove that the production of the bodies, etc. presupposes the action of some intelligent agent? Taken in this sense, however, the argument obviously suffers from the fallacy of redundance or *siddha-sādhana*. It means the effort to prove something which is already admitted by both the parties in a debate or, in more general terms, trying to prove something which is already well-proved even on the admission of the opponent. Hence it is useless to try to prove it over again. Thus, even a staunch atheist (like Kumārila) has nothing to object to the view that the production of the living bodies is due to the actions of the living beings who are intelligent agents. Or, as the Prābhākaras argue in so many words, the living bodies are produced by the actions of the parents, who are, of course, intelligent agents. What, then, is the use of posing an inference to prove this over again? Evidently, therefore, the Nyāya-Vaiśeṣikas cannot take the superintendence or control of the intelligent agent in this wide sense. The same charge of redundance will be advanced against the Nyāya-Vaiśeṣikas if they try to prove the superintendence of an intelligent agent in the sense of some desire being exercised by the intelligent agent. It is admitted by all that the actions of the living beings, which result in the production of the living bodies, are preceded by the desire on the part of these living beings. If, however, the Nyāya-Vaiśeṣikas want to prove that the production of bodies, etc. immediately follow the desire of an intelligent agent, their inference will be totally unacceptable, in as much as there is no instance whatsoever in which the production of anything is found to follow immediately the desire of an intelligent agent. (The jar, for example, is not produced immediately after the potter desires to produce it. This being the typical example on which the Nyāya-Vaiśeṣikas rely, they cannot argue that the bodies, etc. are produced immediately after God desires to produce these.)

To sum up: the intelligent control sought to be proved by the Nyāya-Vaiśeṣikas with the help of their inference can at best prove an intelligent control in the sense in which it is ordinarily observed in everyday life, i.e. the intelligent control by the living beings themselves. However, taken in the sense of creation immediately following the divine desire, the inference is clearly illegitimate.

Secondly, argued Kumārila, the Nyāya-Vaiśeṣikas had to conceive their intelligent agent either as possessing a body or as being without a body. Both the alternatives, were, however, logically untenable and there was no third alternative for them to suggest.

Following Kumārila, let us first take up the possibility of the intelligent agent or God possessing a body. On inferential ground, however, this body of God will have to be viewed as being produced by another intelligent agent. The inference is: God's body must be something produced by an intelligent agent, because it is a body, as for instance, our own bodies. In other words, according to the inference of the Nyāya-Vaiśeṣikas themselves, our own bodies are produced by some intelligent agent because these are made of parts. On the same ground, therefore, the alleged body of God also will have to be considered as produced by an intelligent agent, because, being a body after all, it must be composed of parts.

If the Nyāya-Vaiśeṣikas propose to deny this, their basic inference of the existence of God will become "irregular" *(anaikāntika)* inasmuch as they will have to admit something as being made of parts and yet without being produced by an intelligent agent. In the terminology of Indian logic, any case of the presence of the probans coexisting with the absence of the probandum makes an inference irregular. The denial on the part of the Nyāya-Vaiśeṣikas of God's body being produced by an intelligent cause amounts to the admission of a case of the presence of the probans, namely "made of parts", coexisting with the absence of the probandum, namely "produced by an intelligent agent."

In defence of their own position, however, the Nyāya-Vaiśeṣikas may argue that the divine body is produced by an intelligent cause no doubt, though this intelligent cause is nothing but God himself.

Such a claim obviously amounts to the assertion that God must have been without a body before producing his own body. This leads us to see the absurdity of viewing God as producing something in spite of not possessing a body. God without a body is, in the Nyāya-Vaiśeṣika view, a pure spirit and hence is similar to the liberated souls conceived by the Nyāya-Vaiśeṣikas themselves. But a liberated soul cannot produce anything in the Nyāya-Vaiśeṣika view itself. Thus, in short, God without a body cannot create or produce anything. Hence, there is no question of God creating his own body.

Such, then, was the dilemma of the Nyāya-Vaiśeṣikas: they had to conceive their God either as possessing a body or as being a purely disembodied soul. In the former alternative, there is no possible explanation of His acquiring a body while, in the latter alternative, God—like the liberated soul—cannot be conceived as an agent at all.

Kumārila next explained an incongruity—much more serious from the logical point of view—of the Nyāya-Vaiśeṣika inference of God. This incongruity was that the Nyāya-Vaiśeṣikas had to renounce the very thesis they sought to establish by their inference, if they meant to be serious about the corroborative instance on which their inference vitally depended.

What is the corroborative instance of the Nyāya-Vaiśeṣika inference of God? It is that of the cloth being produced by the weaver or that of the house being built by the mason or, as mentioned most frequently, that of the jar being produced by the potter. For our present purpose, let us keep ourselves confined mainly to the last of these. The jar is made of parts and it is observed to be produced by an intelligent agent in the form of the potter. On the evidence of this, the Nyāya-Vaiśeṣikas argue that all the composite objects of the world must be due to an intelligent cause, which, in the ultimate analysis, can be nothing but God.

But the simple question is: Is the jar really produced by the potter? Or, is the cloth really produced by the weaver and the house by the mason? The Nyāya-Vaiśeṣikas have no alternative other than to answer the question in the affirmative, otherwise they are to deprive their own inference of a corroborative instance while in the standard of Indian logic, an inference without a corroborative instance is quite useless.

However, if the jar is admitted to be something really produced by the potter, God cannot be considered as the creator thereof. Similar must be the cases of the cloth, house, etc. which, if seriously taken as being produced by the weaver, mason, etc. cannot at the same time be regarded as being produced by God. Nevertheless, the Nyāya-Vaiśeṣikas have to admit that the jar is actually produced by the potter, the cloth by the weaver, the house by the mason, and so on. To admit this, however, is absolutely fatal for the Nyāya-Vaiśeṣika inference of God, for it amounts to the surrender of the fundamental thesis of the inference (*sādhya-hīnatā*). The real thesis of the inference is that everything composite in the world is produced by God. The jar, cloth, house, etc. are composite things. If these are admitted to be produced by agents other than God, how can the Nyāya-Vaiśeṣikas at all stick to their main thesis that all the composite objects of the world are made or created by God? Thus, the corroborative instance of the inference, if not lightly taken, calls for the rejection of the very thesis of the inference.

Are, then, the Nyāya-Vaiśeṣikas to surrender the corroborative instance of their inference of God? This, again, is impossible, for the inference itself is impossible without the corroborative instance.

Thus, argued Kumārila, from the logical point of view, the position of the Nyāya-Vaiśeṣikas was not an enviable one. They could not be serious at the same time of their corroborative instance as well as their fundamental thesis. In any case, the Nyāya-Vaiśeṣikas could not agree to give up their corroborative instance, for, as Kumārila argued, this simply meant more troubles for them. As he put it, "if the corroborative instance is taken as valid, there results the pseudo-probans called the contradictory *(viruddha)*, inasmuch as it proves an agent which is not divine and which is perishable, etc." Let us see the implication of this argument.

The corroborative instance is that of the jar produced by the potter. Now, the potter is an intelligent agent no doubt, under whose guidance or superintendence the composite object called the jar is produced. However, what are the characteristic peculiarities of such an intelligent agent? First, it is something purely mundane and not divine. Secondly, it is something essentially perishable and not eternal. If, therefore, the Nyāya-Vaiśeṣikas propose to prove an intelligent cause of all the composite objects of the world on the strength of this corroborative instance, the characteristic peculiarities of the intelligent cause observed in the case of the corroborative instance must be admitted as characterising the intelligent cause inferred of the world. In other words, assuming the validity of the corroborative instance, the only intelligent cause of the world which the Nyāya-Vaiśeṣikas can infer is essentially mundane and perishable, and this flatly contradicts the fundamental thesis of the Nyāya-Vaiśeṣikas, namely a divine and eternal intelligent cause of the world.

Kumārila did not himself consider the possibility of the Nyāya-Vaiśeṣikas defending their own position with the argument that notwithstanding the specific peculiarities of the corroborative instance, what was actually proved by their inference was an intelligent cause in general or a bare intelligent cause. But it is not difficult for us to think how Kumārila could have easily answered such a defence of the inference of God. As against the claim that creation immediately followed the will of God, Kumārila simply argued that there was no instance of production of anything immediately following the desire of an intelligent agent. In the same way Kumārila could have easily dismissed the defence of the Nyāya-Vaiśeṣika position with the argument that there was no instance pointing to the production of anything by an intelligent cause without having any characteristic peculiarity. On the contrary, any corroborative instance that could be mentioned of the intelligent cause producing something was inevitably an instance of an intelligent cause with specific peculiarities like being mundane and perishable. Therefore, any intelligent cause that could be legitimately inferred had to be considered as mundane and perishable.

In view of all these difficulties, asked Kumārila, were the Nyāya-Vaiśeṣikas to surrender their corroborative instance of the potter? This, again, was evidently impossible, for that meant the surrender of their theory of creation altogether. How could the unconscious atoms themselves lead to the creation of the world? In other words, in defence of he theory of creation from unconscious atoms, the Nyāya-Vaiśeṣikas had no alternative other than that of depending on the instance of the potter—the intelligent agent that produced the jar from the intrinsically unconscious materials like clay, etc.

In my previous lecture, I have quoted extensively from Jaimini and Śabara to show how much in details they propose to reject the substantive reality of the Vedic gods and how they propose to look back at them as having no more than sheer verbal values. All this, along with the polemics against the existence of God by the late Mīmāṃsakas, gives us some idea of the religious sentiment among the Vedic priests themselves.

Concluding Remarks

With this rough idea of the priestly ideology as crystallised in the Mīmāṃsā philosophy it is not difficult to understand why it did not—and, as a matter of fact, could not—leave scope for any genuine religious sentiment. The only motivation of the Vedic priests was to attract the rich patrons financing for the sacrifices—the *Yajamāna*-s—so that the priests could get for themselves fat fees—*dakṣiṇā*-s—which was the only source of their livelihood. For this purpose, they had to allure the financiers with all sorts of absurd promises which, the priests argued, were *automatically* assured by the performance of the rituals. Such a view of the essence of the rituals was nothing more than primitive magic, though highly magnified and adorned with all sorts of trivialities to add awe and wonder to these. We have no data, of course, of how many financiers were actually attracted by such claims. From the epics, *purāṇa*-s, etc. we have the impression that there could be a sizeable number of them; even legends of the Upaniṣads—like that of King Janaka of Videha—want us to believe that there were many also in the Upaniṣadic age. However, whatever might have been the actual number of such financiers—big or small—the fact seems to have been that there was a sufficient number of them, because it is difficult to dismiss the entire discussion of the *Dharmaśāstra*-s about the priest class as but a figment of imagination nor is it possible to reject as mere wish-fulfilment the law-makers' dictation that receiving a sacrificial fee or *dakṣiṇā* was the only legitimate source of income for the priests.

In any case, what is of material interest for our present discussion is that the practising Vedic priests refused to take any chance about their own profession even by allowing God or any Vedic deity to interfere with their rituals. They were thus keen on impressing the financiers for the sacrifices that not even the will of God or of any deity could have anything to do with the results assured by the performance of the sacrifices. So God and the deities had to be eliminated in order to make room for a purely magical view of the sacrificial rituals. In doing this they were also obliged to eliminate the most essential function of religion, i.e. to provide people with a palliative remedy for their sufferings. To confront the fact of suffering, people needed a God and also a host of minor deities which they actually had, perhaps partly as inherited from the ancient Harappan Culture, though mostly as their local creations. Thus the word Veda remained as also the vast Vedic literature. But these had little or nothing to contribute to actual religion—or should we say religions—of India, beyond of course some sentences or half-sentences somehow grafted on such of the domestic rituals as *Śrāddha,* etc., which still form the main source of income of the rather impoverished priests today.

What follows from all this is only a simple point. According to the view of the Vedic priests—evidently the foremost custodians of the Vedic tradition—there was nothing that could be called religion in our sense from the Vedic viewpoint. Or, along with what we have already discussed in our lecture IV, the view of God and of gods of the Vedic priests discussed in lectures V and VI, the conclusion we are driven to is that "Vedic religion" is more a myth than reality.

REFERENCE

1. For *Kumārila's atheism Ślokavārtika, Sambandhākṣepaparihāra,* Verses 49 ff.

7

Buddhism: Revolutionary Sociology Passes into its Opposite

1. Preliminary Remarks

The Buddha died at about the age of 80, "probably a few years before or after 485 B.C." The earliest available evidences for the reintroduction of script after the Harappan period being found in the Aśokan inscriptions, it is easily understood why Buddha could not have left for us anything in writing; whatever he preached was orally preached, usually in the form of dialogues. How and when these were committed to writing is still more or less a matter of debate, though the tradition of Ceylon wants us to believe that Aśoka's son "Mahindra actually introduced Buddhism into Ceylon and brought with him the texts of the canon. These texts are said to have been first transmitted orally, until, under the Sinhalese king Vaṭṭagāmini, in the first century B.C., they were committed to writing."[1]

These are in the form of three great collections, and, since the language used in these is Pāli, are usually referred to as the *Pāli Tripiṭaka*-s. How far these actually contain the unmodified teachings of the Buddha we shall probably never know: there are controversies among the practising Buddhists and scholars only with academic interest on this point, which remain inconclusive. However, even admitting later interpolations and perhaps also omissions of the Buddha's teachings in these, it seems that we have no other alternative than to accept their substantial authenticity, for otherwise we shall be left with the only theory that original Buddhism is something unknown and unknowable.

But even admitting the authenticity of the *Pāli Tripiṭaka*-s, there is a sharp controversy among the modern scholars about the actual social affiliation of the Buddha. As Rhys Davids sums it up: "Some writers on Buddhism do not hesitate to ascribe to Gotama the role of a successful political reformer, by representing him as having fought for the poor and despised against the rich and privileged classes, and as having gone far to abolish caste. Other writers gird at the Buddha because most of the leaders of his order were drawn from the ranks of the respectable and the well-to-do, with an education in keeping with their social position: and disparage him for neglecting the humble and the wretched, for not using his influence to abolish, or to mitigate, the harshness of caste rules."[2]

We have quoted this mainly to emphasise one point. Whether original Buddhism was a form of religion in our sense and whether the Buddha had any real taste for philosophy and metaphysics may still be questions open to controversy. However, admitting substantial authenticity of the *Pāli Tripiṭaka*-s there is hardly any scope to doubt that he was about the only thinker in ancient India with an objective interest in sociology, i.e. sociology neither in the sense of the most unscrupulous defence of despotism as we read in the *Arthaśāstra* nor in the sense of fabricating some sort of theological halo for the Brāhmaṇa-Kṣatriya privileges, which we have in the *Dharmaśāstra*-s. The Buddha, for all that we know of him from the *Pāli Tripiṭaka*, was taking at least a precariously near-secular—if not fully secular—sociological interest, judged at least in the context of his time. Further, he was about the only thinker in ancient India with a conscious commitment to the dialectical outlook. Because of this, he also came rather near to the understanding of some "palliative remedy" required by the people in class-divided society. This he formulated in his own way; though, on retrospective analysis, he seems to have anticipated the essential function of religion as understood by Marx. It remains for us to see how, with the adoption of Buddhism as state religion, his original message had to pass into its opposite.

2. Suffering and the Way Out of It

The Buddhist tradition summed up Buddha's own teachings as the Four Noble Truths (*ārya-satya*), with which was linked up the doctrine of the dependent origination of things or *pratītya-samutpāda*. A theory of the chain of 12 causes to explain earthly miseries *(dvādaśā-nidāna)* along with the conception of *nirvāṇa* was, properly speaking, included in the former while from the latter followed the revolutionary views of universal impermanence (*anityatā-vāda*) and of the denial of a permanent soul–substance *(anātma-vāda)*.

The Four Noble Truths were: (1) everything was suffering, (2) suffering had a cause, (3) suffering could be extinguished, and (4) there was a path leading to this extinction. In the famous Sermon at Banaras, these were formulated thus:

> This, O monks, is the sacred truth of suffering: birth is suffering, old age is suffering, sickness is suffering, death is suffering; to be united with the unloved is suffering, to be separated from the loved is suffering; not to obtain what one desires is suffering; in short the five-fold clinging (to the earthly) is suffering.
>
> This, O monks, is the sacred truth of the origin of suffering: it is the thirst (for being) , which leads from birth to birth, together with lust and desire, which finds gratification here and there : The thirst for pleasures, the thirst for being, the thirst for power.
>
> This, O monks, is the sacred truth of the extinction of suffering: the extinction of this thirst by complete annihilation of desire, letting it go, expelling it, separating oneself from it, giving it no room.
>
> This, O monks, is the sacred truth of the path which leads to the extinction of suffering. It is this sacred eight-fold path, to wit: Right Faith, Right Resolve, Right Speech, Right Action,

Right Living, Right Effort, Right Thought, Right Self-concentration. [3]

Everything about these obviously hinged on the first noble truth and the first question about it is: Why was the Buddha so obsessed with the idea that the world was but an ocean of miseries? I have elsewhere tried to answer this question in terms of the tremendous social upheavals of the age. It was the age in which North-East India was first witnessing the rise of the ruthless state-powers—specially those of Magadha and Kośala—on the ruins of the tribal societies. As was characteristic of such an age 'base greed, brutal sensuality, sordid avarice, selfish plunder of common possessions', taxation, usury, extortion and such things were creating new and unheard of miseries in the lives of the people in whose memory the liberty, equality and fraternity of the tribal life was still somewhat fresh and whose neighbours like Mallas, Vajjis and Śākyas were still in the state of tribal simplicity. The Buddha himself belonged to the Śākya tribe and never forgot his tribal pride. But the equality and freedom of the tribes were already threatened because the rising states could not tolerate the continued existence of such examples of democracy, primitive though these might have been. Besides, like deforestation, the expansion of the states required detribalisation of vast areas. Extermination and subjugation of the tribes thus formed the policy- objective of the early states. Vidudabha, the prince of Kośala, presumably during the life of the Buddha, unleashed the most brutal massacre on the Śākyas, the Buddha's own people, and even the children and women of the tribe were not spared. Ajātaśatru, the King of Magadha and one eulogised as a great philosopher in the Upaniṣads, declared, 'I will root out the Vajjians, I will destroy the Vajjians, I will bring these Vajjians to utter ruin'. He even sent his prime minister to the Buddha to seek his blessings for carrying out this determination. The Buddha, with his strong nostalgia for the tribal life, was naturally alarmed by such naked greed for riches and power. "The king", he said, "although he might have conquered the kingdoms of the earth, although he may be the ruler of all land this side of the sea, up to the ocean's shore, would, still insatiate, covet that which is beyond the sea."[5] He could also see how this greed of the kings recoiled back on themselves and made their power and riches unstable. Two of his early patrons were King Bimbisāra of Magadha and King Prasenajit of Kosala. The former was starved to death by his own son Ajātaśatru and the latter most treacherously betrayed by his son Vidudabha. "The princes who rule kingdoms", said the Buddha, "rich in treasures and wealth, turn their greed against one another, pandering insatiably to their desires. If these act thus restlessly, swimming in the stream of impermanence, carried along by greed and carnal desire, who then can walk on earth in peace?"[6] To these were also to be added the hitherto unheard of miseries created in the lives of the people by the new institutions of taxation, slavery, extortion, torture, mortgage, interest, usury: the voluminous *Jātakas* are full of these.

The Buddha himself saw all these. But what was to be done? He was too realistic to believe in any God, prayers and sacrifices to whom could not, he knew, bring any effective remedy to the miseries he saw all around. He did not ask people to pray and sacrifice. In the *Buddhacarita*, Aśvaghoṣa gave elaborate anti-theistic arguments supposed to have been expounded by the Buddha himself. Nor could the Buddha believe in the ascetic self-mortification, which he considered to be 'painful, unworthy and unprofitable.' He was, again, far too disturbed to take seriously the Upaniṣadic claim that the metaphysical wisdom could bring salvation.[7]

He asked his disciples to turn away from 'opinions concerning the beginning and hereafter of things.' For it was no use behaving like a fool who, with an arrow plunged unto his flank, wasted time speculating on the origin, maker, etc., of the arrow, instead of removing it outright. Therefore, when asked metaphysical questions that he considered to be unprofitable, he simply remained silent. In short, the problem that obsessed him most was essentially a practical one. It was the problem of the bewildering mass of sufferings he saw around. And he wanted to have an essentially practical solution for this. But how, under the conditions in which he lived, could such a solution at all be evolved?

There was no question, of course, of really removing the real miseries from this world. That meant skipping over stages of historical development and jumping, as it were, towards socialism which alone, on the basis of the stupendous development of the human productive power, could assure plenty and equality for all. Rather, the further development of the productive power which could eventually ensure such conditions presupposed, during the time of the Buddha, a further intensification of exploitation and all the miseries that it entailed. Therefore, the only alternative left for the prophet was to invent an ideal solution of the real problem and, as a precondition for this, to effect such psychological transformation of the personality in which the sense of the felt misery could be overcome. "A new doctrine", said the Buddha, "do I teach for subduing the mental intoxicants that are generated even in this present life."[8] Elsewhere he said that his purpose was to bring "a quietude of the heart."[9] And how was this to be achieved? Only by inventing the theory and practice of ideology appropriate for his age.

"I have gained coolness", declared the Buddha, "and have attained *nirvāṇa*. To found the Kingdom of Truth, I go to the city of Kasi: I will beat the drum of the immortal in the darkness of the world."[10] But where was this Kingdom of Truth to be found? Significantly, the Buddha did not look forward to what had already emerged and was emerging fuller and fuller every day—the pomp and grandeur of the rising state-powers.

Instead, he looked backward to the tribal collectives and wanted to revive what Marx called 'the imaginary substance of the tribe.' Apparently, he was pleading for a moral reform of the world. In the fourth noble truth, he spoke of right faith, right resolve, etc.,—values, as we can easily judge from the *Jātakas*, that were most ruthlessly trampled upon in the society in which he lived. The Buddha could clearly see the futility of practising all these in the society at large. So he asked the people to take the *pabbajjā* and the *upasampada* ordinations, i.e. 'to go out' of the actual society and 'to arrive at' the life of the *saṃgha*-s or the order of the monks. For within the *saṃgha*-s, things were different. Modelled consciously on the tribal collectives—without private property and with full equality and democracy among the brethren—these alone could offer the real scope to practise the 'simple moral grandeur of the ancient gentile society', for which the Buddha was really pleading. Thus the *saṃgha*-s, as classless societies within the bosom of the class society, could become the heart of a heartless world, the spirit of a spiritless situation.

3. Buddha's Sociology and Dialectics

We may now pass on to have some more idea of the sociology of the Buddha—particularly his view of private property, the social classes and the state which—it is perhaps not an accident—directly follows from his dialectical outlook.

For understanding his sociology as following from his dialectical outlook, it may be convenient to begin this discussion with an observation of Stcherbatsky, where he shows the radical implications on the question of private property as connected with the radical view of personality in early Buddhism.

> Where there is personality, there is property belonging to it. Where there is I, there is also my. And where there is personal property, there necessarily emerges a love for it in one form or other. This attachment to personal property is the root of all evil, the root of every personal action as well as of social injustice. Thus, by negating the existence of the soul, Buddhism gives us a very profound philosophical basis for the negation of the right of personal property.
>
> What personal property can be possible where even the

> personality itself is not there? Therefore, a real Buddhist is only he who has renounced personal property—and not merely property but also family, home, etc.—once for all. In the history of world religions, of Christianity and Islam, we frequently find doctrines which negate property and advise that this be renounced. But Buddhism gives the most radical treatment of this question.[11]

However, let us not see in the Buddha's condemnation of private property more significance than it has. It is nothing, for example, comparable to the demand for the abolition of the private ownership of the means of production as an essential precondition for the positive emancipation of man, which is above all an emancipation from class exploitation and therefore possible only by the overthrow of the class structure of society. Not to speak of this, Buddhism never comes anywhere near the positive conception of freedom, viz. freedom as attainable only by a greater mastery over nature based on a deeper insight into it and its laws. Such an understanding of freedom could not be developed during the Buddha's times. What was historically possible for him was to work out some palliative remedy for suffering, which he saw everywhere and in everything. All that he could suggest was to change the subjective attitude to the world—to subdue the 'mental intoxicants' and thereby to attain 'a quietude of the heart.' Private property is to be renounced because, as the Buddha feels, it creates these mental intoxicants—longing, clinging, attachment, and so on. The view of the unreality of personality, he thinks, helps one to realise the foolishness of pursuing personal property and is thus an incentive to renounce private property.

But private property, as the Buddha understands it, is to be avoided within the *saṃgha*–s or communities of the monks. These monks are supposed to renounce the world, which in fact means that they are supposed to leave the world as it is. It is beyond the power of the prophet to interfere: with the inexorable laws of history, which, during the Buddha's times, required a greater intensification of private property in the hands of the despots, monarchs and merchants. This is one example of what we call "the dialectic of progress."

The Buddha's demand for the abolition of private property is a demand for its abolition within the isolated pockets of society and it is not—what would have been historically premature—the demand for the abolition of private property from society as such. As the Buddha himself advises the brotherhood of monks:

> Live as islands unto yourselves, brethren, as refuges unto yourselves; take none other as your refuge; live with the Norm as your island, with the Norm as your refuge; take none other as your refuge.
>
> But how does a brother live in an island unto himself, as a refuge unto himself, taking none other as his refuge? How does he live with the Norm as his island, with the Norm as his refuge, taking none other as his refuge?
>
> Herein a brother, as to the body, as to feelings, as to thought, as to ideas, continues so to look upon these that he remains ardent, self-possessed and mindful, that he may overcome both the hankering and the dejection common in the world. Thus it is, brethren, that a brother lives as an island and as a refuge unto himself... with the Norm as an island and as a refuge, having no other refuge.[12]

So it will be an error to make of the Buddha a revolutionary in our sense of the term. At the same time, it will be another error not to see what is actually revolutionary about his sociology—particularly in so far as it follows from his dialectical outlook—his view of everything being involved in perpetual flux.

The passage just quoted forms the concluding sermon of a dialogue the whole of which is designed to discuss the question of wealth, and of wickedness, aggressiveness and war as following from it. A superficial reading of the dialogue as a whole may give one the impression of a fairy tale as it were—the dream of a golden age in the past and the fall of man from it with the growth of wealth and hence also of the greed for wealth. But that would be misunderstanding the dialogue, or the main point sought to be emphasised in it by the Buddha in his own way.

Equipped with no tool for socio-historical analysis in our sense—or, more strictly, possessing the only tool in the form of his intuitive vision of the dialectical outlook—the Buddha is trying nevertheless to understand and explain a momentous historical question, the question of the origin of wealth which, as he understands, creates wickedness, aggressiveness and war. And what is revolutionary about his understanding is not merely the total absence of any supernatural cant about the phenomena—and therefore that total absence of any tendency to invest them with any supernatural sanction as in the *puruṣasūkta* of the *Ṛgveda*, the *Brāhmaṇa*-s, *Upaniṣad*-s and above all in the *Dharmaśāstra*-s —but the view that like everything else in the universe, wealth and the consequent aggressiveness and war, are subject to the relentless law of *pratītya-samutapāda*: all these come into being subject to the collocation of a number of definite conditions and hence these are also destined to pass away.

From this point of view, Stcherbatsky's suggestion that the Buddha's rejection of private property is only a corollary of his rejection of soul and personal property, perhaps needs amendment. Still, in the Buddha's thoughts the rejection of the two is not unconnected. The soul is unreal, because there is nothing but perpetual flux—the coming into being and passing away. But so also is the power of wealth and private property. Like the soul and personality, private property too is subject to the relentless law of *pratītya-samutpāda*, which is the theoretical ground of the view of universal flux. It is, of course, understandable that the Buddha has to grope for expressions for the formulation of such a momentous idea. And the expressions he uses cannot but appear to us to be rather archaic. As Buddha is said to have preached:

> Thus brethren, from goods not being bestowed on the destitute, poverty grew great... stealing, violence, murder, lying, evil speaking, adultery, abusive and idle talk, covetousness and

ill–will, false opinion, incest, wanton greed and perverted lust.... Among the humans, brethren, keen mutual enmity will become the rule—keen ill-will, keen animosity, passionate thought even of killing, in a mother towards her child, in a child towards its mother, in a father towards his child and a child towards its father, in brother to brother, in brother to sister, in sister to brother. Just as a sportsman feels towards the game that he sees, so will they feel.

Among such humans, brethren there will arise a sword- period of seven days, during which they will look at each other as wild beasts; sharp swords will appear ready to their hands and they, thinking—This is a wild beast, 'This is a wild beast'—will with their swords deprive each other of life.

Then to some of those beings it will occur: Let us not slay just anyone; nor let just anyone slay us!..... Then this, brethren, will occur to those beings: Now only because we had gotten into evil ways, have we had this heavy loss of kith and kin. Let us now therefore do good. What can we do that is good? Let us now abstain from taking life. That is a good thing that we may take up and do. And they will abstain from slaughter, and will continue in this good way....

At that period, brethren, there will arise in the world an Exalted one named Metteyyà (?Maitreya), an *arhat*, fully awakened, abounding in wisdom and goodness, happy, with knowledge of the worlds, unsurpassed as a guide to mortals willing to be led, a teacher for gods and men, an exalted one, a Buddha, even as I am now. He, by himself, will thoroughly know and see, as it were face to face, this universe, with its world of the spirits, its Brahmās and its Māras, and its world of recluses and Brahmins, of princes and peoples, even as I see now, by myself, thoroughly know and see them. The truth, lovely in its origin, lovely in its progress, lovely in its consummation, will he proclaim both in the spirit and in the letter, the higher life will he make known, in all its fullness and in all its purity, even as I do now.

He will be accompanied by a congregation of some thousands of brethren, even as I am now accompanied by a congregation of some hundreds of brethren.[13]

What is definite about all this is that the Buddha is not prophesying the coming of a leader to organise a revolutionary party for the final overthrow of a society every fabric of which is permeated with evil—evil that originally follows from the accumulation of wealth or private possession, or, as the Buddha puts, it, from 'goods not being bestowed on the destitute'. The Buddha never visualises a revolutionary trasformation of society. Nevertheless, the origin of social evil and its eventual passing away, as he understands the entire process, cannot be looked at as a mere phantasy or a mythological imagination of the fall of man from an original golden age awaiting some ultimate salvation by a future messiah. Not that such elements are not at all there in the Buddha's thought. Still, what is decisive about his thought is the vision of the law of universal causation—*pratītya-samutpāda*—the inescapable consequence of which is the view of universal flux. In accordance with this, the Buddha is trying to understand society, which he feels is permeated with greed, aggressiveness and evil in other forms. But he is also obliged to conceive its coming into being and its eventual destiny of passing away. What is significant about his understanding of social evil is not the way in which he conceives its origin and its passing away. It is rather his general theoretical position that, like everything else in the universe, social evil must itself be involved in the universal flux: it cannot but come into existence subject to definite conditions and it cannot but ultimately pass away.

Its coming into being, as far as he can trace it, is connected with wealth or private possession; but its passing away can be conceived by him only in terms of moral revival under the leadership of a great enlightened saint. This—particularly the second point—is of course the result of the inevitable historical limitations. But the basic theoretical position that there is nothing eternal about the social organisation—that everything in it has a definite beginning and therefore also a definite end—is a remarkable achievement of the dialectical outlook of early Buddhism.

And this cannot but be reminiscent of Morgan's verdict on society based on private property, with which Engels concludes his work on *The Origin of the Family, Private Property and the State:*

> A mere property career is not the final destiny of mankind, if progress is to be the law of the future as it has been of the past. The time which has passed away since civilisation began is but a fragment of the past duration of man's existence, and but a fragment of the ages yet to come. The dissolution of society bids fair to become the termination of a career of which property is the end and aim, because such a career contains the elements of self-destruction.[14]

It is no use speculating whether, given modern terminologies, the Buddha would have formulated his verdict on property-oriented society in the same way. The fact is that modern terminologies are not there for him. Nevertheless, what is there for him—and the importance of which can in no way be overlooked—is the dialectical view, the relentless law of *praṭītya-samutpāda*. This leads him to express, in his own way, the view that mere property career cannot be the final destiny of mankind: it comes into being subject to definite conditions and it is foredoomed to wither away.

In another dialogue forming part of the early canonical literature of the Buddhists, the implications of the dialectical outlook for the Buddha's sociology are worked out in a more remarkable manner. The main point of this dialogue—called the *Aggañña Suttanta*—is to explain not only the origin of kingship but the broader question of the origin of the main strata of traditional Indian society—the four traditional castes. As the Buddha is trying to explain, such society comes into being because of a number of specific conditions, and the inevitable consequence of this is that, because of the same relentless law of *partītya-samutpāda,* such a society is also destined to pass away. This significance of the dialogue may be entirely missed if we try to assess, in terms of contemporary sociology, the intrinsic worth of the Buddha's view of the origin of caste-oriented society. Weaker still is the Buddha's visualisation of the mode of the eventual passing away of this society: he can at best speak of his own *saṃgha*-s within which the rigidity of the castes is supposed to dissolve. However, all these are not the points by which we are to judge the basic significance of the sociology of early Buddhism. This significance is to be sought elsewhere, and that is the view that, like everything else in the universe, the caste-oriented society too comes into being only under certain specific conditions and hence it is also destined to pass away.

Before passing on to see how the Buddha expresses his own view of the caste-oriented society, it may be convenient to remember the other view then in circulation, i.e. the view sought to be negated by the Buddha. From the times of the *puruṣa-sūkta* of the *Ṛgveda*, the *Brāhmaṇa*-s and *Upaniṣad*-s, there develops the zeal to sanctify the caste-oriented society by claiming for it a divine origin. And since it is supposed to be divine creation, it is impossible—and of course impious—to try to change its basic structure. The caste-oriented society, in other words, is beyond the range of change altogether: if it has an origin in the divine will, the same will give it life eternal. It would be tedious to quote the passages from the *Brāhmaṇa*-s and *Upaniṣad*-s to show how such a view of the essential unalterableness of caste society takes shape, though finally in the *Dharmaśāstra*. But it may be sufficient for our purpose to quote a few couplets from Manu, in whose legal codes is summed up the Brahmanical view of the caste society with the divine sanction for it. As Manu puts it, "But in order to protect this universe, He, the most resplendent one, assigned separate duties and occupations to those who sprang from his mouth, arms, things and feet. To Brahmins He assigned teaching and studying (the Veda), sacrificing for their own benefit and of others, giving and accepting (of gifts). The Kṣatriya He commanded to protect the people, to bestow gifts, to offer sacrifices, to study (the Veda) and to abstain from attaching himself to sensual pleasures; the Vaiśya to tend cattle, to bestow gifts, to offer sacrifices, to study (the Veda), to trade, to lend money and to cultivate land. One occupation only the Lord prescribed to the Śūdra—to serve meekly even these three (other) castes."[15]

Such a view, though codified by Manu at a comparatively later date, comes down from distant antiquity and is fully known to the Buddha. The Brahmin Vāśettha tells him how the Brahmins themselves claim to prove their superiority: "Only the Brahmins are genuine children of Brahmā, born of his mouth, offspring of Brahmā, created by Brahmā, heirs of Brahmā." But the Buddha laughs at the *prima facie* absurdity of such a claim: "Surely, Vāśettha, the Brahmins have quite forgotten the past when they say so? On the contrary, the Brāhmaṇīs, the wives of Brahmins, are known to be fertile, are seen to be with child, bringing forth and nursing children. And yet it is these very womb-born Brahmins who say that.....Brahmins are genuine children of Brahmā, born from his mouth, his offspring, his creation and his heirs."[16]

Thus the ground on which the Brahmins want to prove their social superiority is to the Buddha a mere myth. Still the fact of the caste-divided society is there: "There are these four classes, Vāśettha, nobles, Brahmins, tradesfolk, work people."[17] And that needs an explanation. I have elsewhere quoted this dialogue extensively[18] and need not repeat it over again. But the essentially secular view taken in it is in need of reemphasis. So also the dialectical understanding underlying the whole discussion.

In this dialogue, the Buddha wants us to understand the origin of these social classes out of an originally homogeneous community of beings as a purely natural phenomenon, or, according to the Buddhist way of putting it, due to the operation of the universal law of causation, of *pratītya-samutpāda*. However, in the same Buddhist view, there is also the other side of the same law: anything that comes into being is also destined to pass away. The veil, once lifted on the past, also reveals a future. If caste-society comes into being subject to definite conditions, because of the instability of these conditions it is also destined to wither away. This is the revolutionary implication of the sociology of early Buddhism—an implication that inevitably follows from the view of universal flux—though it is also the severest historical limitation of the Buddha himself to have failed to visualise how exactly this caste-society is going to wither away. Still the implication is there and the Buddha is obliged to work it out.

The only way he finds it possible to work it out is to talk of his *saṃgha*-s—the pockets of classless society created by him within the general structure of class society of his times—within which the distinction of castes does not exist, thanks to the general technique of changing the subjective attitude to reality which, as he imagines, is conducive to freedom. This is an illusion no doubt. But it is also a historically inevitable limitation. Thus after elaborately describing how caste society comes into being, the Buddha describes as follows how it is going to pass away, though only within the brotherhood of monks:

> Again, Vāśettha, a Kṣatriya,....a Brahmin too... Vaiśya too... a Śūdra too, who is self-restrained in deed, word and thought, and has followed after the practice of the seven principles which are the 'wings of wisdom', attains to complete extinction of evil in this present life.
>
> For, Vāśettha, whosoever of these four classes becomes, as a *bhikṣu*, an *arhat*, who has destroyed the intoxicants, who has done that which is behoved him to do, who has laid down the burden, who has won his own salvation, who has wholly destroyed the fetter of rebirth, who through knowledge made perfect is free—he is declared chief among them, in virtue of a norm.[19]

Such then is the vision of the withering away of caste-society that the Buddha can have. This is the destiny of the dialectical outlook being extended to the understanding of society under conditions that are historically premature for the full working out of the dialectics of social transformation. However, as we have already said, the real significance of the Buddha's sociology is not to be sought in the way in which he visualises its withering away but in his general verdict on caste society. And this verdict is that like everything else in the universe, caste-society itself is nothing more than a passing phase. In this sense early Buddhism does mean a condemnation of the norm of caste society which, according to the spokesmen of the norm itself, is nothing if it has no eternal verity with a divine sanction.

4. Buddhism Becoming A State Religion

If the Buddha pronounced a devastating condemnation of private property and looked at it as the source of all evils and sufferings, private property took its revenge posthumously, as it were, on the Buddha and his teachings. For historically speaking, the fact is that specially from the time of Aśoka Buddhism started thriving more and more on the financial and political support of the monarchs, feudatory chiefs, wealthy merchants and other rich patrons, and the more it did so the more it was obliged to follow the obvious logic that he who pays the pipers calls for the tune. The metamorphosis in Buddhism was so great that it eventually had to assume a new name for it which was Mahāyāna, and which sought to justify its claim to be Buddhism proper by the fabrication of a whole host of new "scriptures", broadly called the *Mahāyāna-sūtra*-s with the story that Buddha himself wrote these, though considering that it would have been premature to preach these in his own times, kept these concealed among the Nagas, so that many centuries later, Nagarjuna was to discover these. Here is how Stcherbatsky describes the change:

> When we see an atheistic, soul-denying philosophic teaching of a path to personal Final Deliverance, consisting in an absolute extinction of life and a simple worship of the memory of its human founder—when we see it superseded by a magnificent High Church with a Supreme God, surrounded by a numerous pantheon and a host of saints, a religion highly devotional, highly ceremonious and clerical, with an ideal of Universal

> Salvation of all living creatures, a Salvation by the divine grace of the Buddhas and the Bodhisattvas, a Salvation not in annihilation, but in eternal life,—we are fully justified in maintaining that the history of religions has scarcely witnessed such a break between the new and the old within the pale of what nevertheless continues to claim common descent from the same religious founder.[20]

We do not obviously have the scope here to discuss the entire history of the subsequent development of Buddhism. But it is necessary for our purpose to have some idea of its salient points.

The first casualty of the new Buddhism which announces itself as the Mahāyāna is the Buddha himself, the memory of whose historicity is sought to be washed away with a flood of new mythology—the theory of the Buddhas and Bodhisattvas or future Buddhas. Its second casualty is the atheism of the Buddha, which, though not formally rejected, is in fact substituted by the creed of a supreme god placed at the top of a mixed pantheon of smaller deities and hobgoblins. Its third casualty is the Buddha's expressed distaste for metaphysics, now replaced by a spurt of metaphysical exuberance. One aspect of this is the tendency to develop into an extreme form of world-denying idealism. The other aspect of this is the growing resistance to the dialectical outlook—a resistance that reaches its philosophical climax in the Śūnya- vāda of Nāgārjuna.

But before we pass on to see the philosophical expression of this resistance, it is interesting to note how, in the scriptural work fabricated by the Mahāyānists, is codified the rejection of the dialectical outlook in its sociological aspect.

In early Buddhism, like everything else, kingship too comes into being because of some specific natural conditions. What inevitably follows from the general formula of *pratītya-samutpāda* is quite simple. Kingship, because it has a definite origin, has also a definite end.

Understandably enough, is becomes eventually impossible for Buddhism to retain such an attitude to the kings, on whose patronage that creed is increasingly dependent. The attitude to kingship has to be revised and revised in a direction that best suits the patrons of Buddhism. Accordingly, in the Mahāyāńa scriptures, the king is viewed as a son of god and kingship is invested with a divine sanction. Thus, in the *Suvarṇaprabhāsottama sūtra*, the god Brahmā is brought to declare:

> How does a king, who is born of men, come to be called divine?
>
> Why is the king called the son of the gods?
>
> If a king is born in this world of mortals
>
> How can it be that a god rules over men?
>
> I will tell you of the origin of kings, who are born in the world of mortals, and for what reason kings exist, and rule over every province. By the authority of the great gods a king enters his mother's bomb. First he is ordained by gods–only then does he find an embryo, What though he is born or dies in the world of mortals—Arising from the gods he is called the son of gods. The thirty–three great gods assign the fortune of the king. The ruler of the men is created as the son of all the gods. To put a stop to unrighteousness, to prevent evil deeds, to establish all beings in well-doing, and to show them the way to heaven. Whether men, or god, or fairy, or demon, or outcaste—he is a true king who prevents evil deeds. Such a king is mother and father to those who do good. He was appointed by gods to show the results of *karma*.[21]

The Mahāyāna scripture just quoted is written—or, according to the pontifical expression permitted by Mahāyānists, 'came to the world'—several centuries after the Buddha. The divine origin of and divine sanction for kingship proclaimed in it are not just an ad hoc ideological grant to the great patrons of Buddhism. It is rather a symptom of the serious ideological retreat of later Buddhism—a retreat resulting from its ever-growing parasitism. In the context of our present discussion, we shall note only one aspect of this retreat, i.e. the retreat from the dialectical outlook of original Buddhism.

One expression of the tendency to flout the Buddha's view of universal flux is to reinstate the concept of soul in Buddhist philosophy. We are told that this is one of the issues that leads to the first split among the Buddhists. "The *Kathāvatthu* begins its exposition of divergent views by a long discussion of the question about the possible reality of the soul. The schools of *Ārya-Sammitīyas* and *Vātsiputrīyas* were inclined to interpret the doctrine of soullessness in a sense which admitted some, albeit very feeble, unity in the elements of personality."[22]

Understandably, much of this new controversy is scripture-oriented. Not only do the contending parties try to reinterpret the words of the Buddha in their own way; there is moreover the zeal to own or disown certain statements as genuine words of the Buddha. Thus the older or orthodox Buddhists, usually called the Theravādins, accuse the Vātsiputrīya of having suppressed the scriptural passages that go against their views, while the Vātsiputrīyas, in their turn, accuse the Theravādins of leaning upon passages that were not genuinely scriptural.[23] However, scriptures apart, some of the grounds mentioned by the Vātsiputrīyas in defence of their view of a somewhat shadowy but permanent soul are intended to be logical. For example, they argue that the fact of memory cannot be explained without the admission of a soul—an argument which in the comparatively later period is specially advanced by the Nyāya Vaiśeṣikas:

> Now, if there is absolutely no soul, how is it then that the detached moments of consciousness can remember or recognise things which had been experienced a long time ago? .... If there were absolutely nothing permanent, it would mean that one consciousness had perceived the object and another one remembers it. How is it possible? In this case, things experienced by Devadatta's consciousness would be remembered by the consciousness of Yajñadatta.... If there is no soul, whose is the recollection, whom does it belong to?[24]

There is moreover the evidence of the cognising agent on

which the Vātsiputrīyas are said to depend:

> A soul must exist, because wherever there is an activity it depends on an agent. Every action depends on an agent. Thus, in the example 'Devadatta walks', there is an action of walking which depends on Devadatta, the agent. To be conscious is likewise an action. Hence the agent who cognises must also exist.[25]

But the Vātsiputrīyas apparently hesitate to revive the concept of the permanent soul in the full sense of the term: "But in our opinion, the self means that the individual is neither one of the elements, nor is it something outside the elements."[26] Moreover, there is really no ground to think that such a hesitant step towards the reintroduction of the soul into Buddhist philosophy meets with any great success.

What we hear of them is from others—i.e. the rival Buddhists—who are moreover keen mainly on ridiculing the Vātsiputrīyas.

After the Vātsiputrīyas, the early Vijñāna-vādins make a comparatively bolder attempt at what Stcherbatsky has described as "a disguised return from the theory of stream of thought of the doctrine of a substantial soul."[27] This is expressed as their views of *ālaya-vijñāna* and *tathāgata-garbha*, of which the former is more philosophical, the latter frankly mythologico-metaphysical.

The concept of *ālaya-vijñāna* means something like the 'all conserving mind'—'a store-house, a real granary, where the seeds *(bīja)* or all future ideas and the traces of all past deeds are stored up'.[28] According to Vallée Poussin, "The *ālaya-vijñāna* is somewhat like a soul, and we know from the Tibetan authorities that the maintainers of the Hīnayāna strongly objected to this new vijñāna. It is a series of 'subliminal images'—a store of seeds that give birth to actual cognitions; it may be looked upon as a thinking entity which manifests itself in a succession of thoughts."[29]

The concept is specially emphasised by Aśvaghoṣa, who may be the same as the author of the famous *Buddhacarita* and who, we are further told, "was summoned to Kabul by Kātyāyanīputra, the alleged composer of the 'Abhidharma in Eight Sections', in order to help him in the compilation of the Great Commentary *(Mahāvibhāṣā)* on the text of Abhidharma," i.e. to help the grand metaphysical activity said to have taken place in the Council convened under the patronage of king Kaṇiṣka.

But the concept of *ālaya-vijñāna* has a prominent place also in Vijñānavāda as expounded by Asaṅga. In his philosophy, it means something precariously near the Upaniṣadic soul from which the entire complex of subjective and objective world is supposed to emanate, as Anesaki has shown.[30]

Much more peculiar is the concept of the *tathāgata-garbha,* under the cover of which practically the old Upaniṣadic concept of one eternal soul as embedded in all individual souls is sought to be smuggled in by Mahāyāna Buddhists. For understanding this concept, we have first to note the quaint transformation of the idea of the Tathāgata in Mahāyāna Buddhism. In early Buddhism, Tathāgata is simply an epithet of the historical Buddha and it means one who has gone beyond the sphere of worldly attachments or, more simply, one who has attained wisdom. In the mystical mythologies fabricated by the Mahāyānists, however, the concept of the Tathāgata is invested with an altogether new significance. It represents some kind of transcendental metaphysical reality from which all the Buddhas and Bodhisattvas are imagined to emanate or appear as *avatāra*-s. These Buddhas and future Buddhas have their histories; but the Tathāgata as such is supposed to be an eternal personality without any extinction. One of the *Mahāyāna* scriptures called the *Saddharma-puṇḍarīka* dilates much on the cumbrous theology of the eternal personality—of the Upaniṣadic soul—woven round the concept of the Tathāgata. But it will be tedious for the readers to go even through extracts from the text. The essential point, however, is that with a good deal of mumbo-jumbo, this Māhāyāna "scripture" wants to smuggle in into Buddhism, the essential features of the Upaniṣadic conception of a permanent soul or *ātma* which was unceremoniously discarded by early Buddhism.

Apparently all that is much too complicated to be readily understood by the common people. For the purpose of mass consumption, therefore, the need is felt for a more popular version of basically the same view. The Mahāyāna Buddhists hope to achieve this by identifying their Tathāgata with god Amitābha, the lord of Sukhāvatī, or with god Vairocana, and all this the people were asked to believe to be the same as the theory of soullessness of Buddhism. This represents the final theological version of the retreat from the dialectical outlook of original Buddhism, an outlook which is usually expressed as *anātma-vāda* or the theory of soullessness.

The theory completely passes into its opposite when it becomes the cult of a personal god. "Soullessness", Stcherbatsky observes, "was later on conceived in a pantheistic sense and personified as the primeval Buddha Vairocana. The same can be maintained with regard to its theistic conception personified as Buddha Amitābha, whose worship gave rise to the new religion."[31]

Such are some of the features of the ideological retreat of Mahāyāna Buddhism. Flouting the original view of universal flux, it pleads for divine sanction and therefore of unalterability of kingship. It wants to readapt the conception of the soul, first somewhat vaguely by the Vātsiputrīyas, then in the more well- defined form as the *ālaya-vijñāna* of the early Vijñāna-vādins, and finally in their quaint metaphysico-mythological conception of *tathāgata garbha*. At the same time it completely repudiates the atheism of the Buddha and preaches the cult of a personal god, identifying it mystically with soullessness as ultimate reality.

5. Concluding Remarks

We have now some idea of how in the Mahāyāna Buddhism the really revolutionary sting of the Buddha's original teaching—specially his sociology and dialectical outlook—

was practically removed, and rooms were made in the new cumbrous theology for the reintroduction of many a major factor of the official ideology intended to be rejected by the Buddha himself. Along with the internal ideological changes, there took place also external changes in the rituals of Buddhism, making it practically indistinguishable from official Hinduism. For having some idea of this we may turn to Tārānātha, the Tibetan historian of Indian Buddhism, on whom the modern historians specially of the Pāla period are obliged to depend.

He left for us, though in his own way, clear indications of the factors that contributed to the decline and fall of Buddhism in India. Buddhism, in its latest phase, as Tārānātha so vividly described it,[32] almost completely surrendered precisely to those beliefs and practices, as a direct rejection of which the Buddha himself had preached his original creed. For all we know, it was a creed concerned above all with the fact of suffering, and with the way out of suffering. As Stcherbatsky puts it, "It can hardly be said to represent a religion. Its more religious side, the teaching of a path is utterly human. Man reaches salvation by his own efforts through moral and intellectual perfection. Nor was there, for aught we know, very much of a worship in the Buddhism of that time. The community consisted or recluses possessing neither family nor property, assembling twice a month for open confession of their sins and engaged in the practice of austerity, meditation and philosophic discussions." The Buddha preached all these precisely because he had realised the futility of worshipping God or a host of demi-gods, offering sacrifices to them or trying to coerce them with magical rituals. For the Buddha himself these beliefs and practices were characteristics of the *tirthika*-s or outsiders. By contrast, Buddhism in its latest phase—if we are to trust Tārānātha—bowed down to all these beliefs and thus became practically indistinguishable from popular Hinduism, so-called. It assumed the form of being an elaborate worship of all sorts of gods and goddesses of the popular pantheon—often under new names, but sometimes caring not even to invent any new name for them—and of indulging in all sorts of ritual practices of which the Buddha himself had expressed his unambiguous repulsion.

Thus, e.g. the Vikramaśīla-Vihāra, the last grand centre of Buddhism established in India, had even the provision for a Bali-ācārya and a Homa-ācārya! Buddhajñāpāda, Tārānātha further tells us, persuaded King Dharmapāla to perform a *homa* of many years, during which period the king spent over nine lakh and two thousand *tolā*-s of silver—and all these were designed to make his dynasty last longer! And so on. Evidently, the memory of the human founder of the creed and even the vestige of his essentially human teachings were fully lost to the Buddhists and their patrons when Buddhism assumed such a queer form. The ideology, in short, passed into its opposite, and being left with no internal justification to survive as a distinct creed, the only thing on which it could then thrive was the fad of some big patron, the Pālas being about the last of them. With the withdrawal or collapse of this patronage, Buddhism had to go into pieces.

Sharing fully the creed in its latest phase, Tārānātha is of course not expected to have realised all these. As far as he understood, therefore, the end of the Vikramaśīla and the Odantapuri meant the end of Buddhism in India: with the fall of these two monasteries the Buddhist *ācārya*-s ran hither and thither, seeking shelter in Kashmir, Nepal and the Ko-ki countries. He does not ask himself how a creed can, so long as it possesses any inner vitality, become virtually extinct form such a vast country only with the fall of two centres situated somewhere in Bihar.

Such then is a possible account of the decline and end of Buddhism in the country of its birth. But the story of Buddhism does not end here. In some of the neighbouring countries—specially Tibet and Mongolia—the rising monarchical power found in the new Buddhism a very suitable ideology, not only providing with the most suitable palliative for suffering masses but also to keep them cowed with awe, wonder and fear. Thus the Tibetan historians of Tibet—who themselves profess to be devout Mahāyānists—tell us with tremendous enthusiasm about the zeal of the Tibetan monarchs to suppress the older religion of Tibet—called Bon (pronounced as Pan)—and establish Mahāyāna Buddhism as the state religion of the country. Though this is a different story altogether, we should like to add only one point to it. The Tibetan monarchs would not certainly have been so enthusiastic about the religious reform of Tibet if they did not sense in it a distinct political function.

This introduces us to another aspect of religion, namely its political function, which we propose to discuss more fully in the next lecture.

REFERENCES

1. M. Winternitz ii. 8.
2. T.W. Rhys Davids DB. i. 96.
3. Tr. H. Oldenberg BHLHTHO 128-29.
4. D. Chattopadhyaya L 459 ff; IP 122 ff.
5. Quoted by Oldenberg, *op. cit.* 64.
6. *Ibid.*
7. This is the usual view of early Buddhism accepted by modern scholars.
8. Quoted by Gaden in SBE xiii. 84-5.
9. *Ibid.*
10. *Ibid.* xiii. 91.
11. Th. Stcherbatsky FPS 26.
12. T.W. Rhys Davids DB iv. 74-5
13. T.W. Rhys Davids DB iv. 69-74.
14. Quoted by Engels OF 291-2.
15. Manu i. 87-91.
16. T.W. Rhys Davids DB iv. 78.
17. *ib.* iv. 79.
18. D. Chattopadhyaya WLWDIP 527 ff.
19. T.W. Rhys Davids DB iv. 93.
20. Th. Stcherbatsky CBN 33.
21. Quoted by de Bary 185-86.
22. Th. Stcherbatsky STB 5.
23. Th. Stcherbatsky CCB 4n & STB 33.

24. Th. Stcherbatsky STB 62.
25. *Ib.* 62.
26. *Ib. 34.*
27. Th. Stcherbatsky CBN 53.
28. *Ib.* 52.
29. Vallé Poussin in ERE ix. 851-2.
30. Anesaki in ERE ii. 62.
31. Th. Stcherbatsky STB 6.
32. For details given from *Tārānātha,* See summary of these in the introduction to THBI (ed. D. Chattopadhyaya).

8

Future of Religion

1. Preliminary Remarks

In this concluding lecture, I shall try to sum up the main point I have been trying to argue. The argument is that everything in the universe—both material and spiritual—is involved in the process of coming into existence and passing out of existence or the process of ceaseless flux. This is the essence of the dialectical method of Hegel which, as shorn of its mysticism and idealistic fantasy of Hegel himself, is accepted by Marxism as forming one of its most important components. Applying this method to the phenomenon called religion, the essential point resolves into the following.

Religion once came into being as necessarily as it is destined to pass away. In other words, for the convenience of discussion, the proposition can be split into two sub-propositions. First, religion has a definite beginning. Secondly, it has no future other than that of withering away. The first sub-proposition we have tried to substantiate in two steps. One of these is to show that there was a period when human beings were unaware of anything that we call religion. This was the period of the primitive pre-class society. The savages still surviving in certain pockets of the world and uncontaminated by the merchants and missionaries penetrating into them, have no religion. Instead of religion they rely on magic. Similarly, wherever we can successfully go back to the prehistory of civilised society, we come across magic instead of religion. For many thousands of years—how many we are yet to know precisely—man remained in such a stage of pre-class society, and this because of the extremely low level of the technique of production. The utmost labour of the entire community was required to maintain it at the minimum level of subsistence. There was no surplus and therefore no possibility of one section of the community living on the labour of another. At such a helpless stage of depending on the most rudimentary productive capacity, man felt the need for supplementing his actual technique by an illusory one, and that was magic.

In his struggle against nature, however, man was not destined to remain at such a helpless stage. He went on developing his tools of production, at first slowly—almost imperceptibly slowly—though after many thousand years, he took steps towards what the archaeologists call the neolithic revolution. From this stage onwards, the pace of human progress acquired spectacular momentum. Thanks to the improved technique of production, man eventually acquired the capacity of producing more than was necessary for his bare maintenance. In other words, he started producing surplus. When this took place, man reached a stage which can be described as the first foreshadowing of civilisation. But not yet civilisation proper. For the purpose of moving forward to civilisation, a further revolution was necessary, for which Gordon Childe used the descriptive epithet "the urban revolution". The most essential pre-condition for this revolution was the channelisation of the social surplus of the direct producers—mainly the farmers and peasants—to certain centres, which, when we look back at these, appear to be incipient cities. Without the accumulation of social surplus in these centres, there was no possibility of having whole-time specialists engaged in vairous arts and crafts who, as whole-timers, could no longer act also as the producers of their own means of subsistence. And without whole-time specialists there could not be the urban revolution. Some machinery was thus needed for the channelisation of the social surplus to the incipient city centres. We have argued that of all the conceivable machineries for the purpose, the one that was most feasible and least cumbrous must have been the creation of an ideological device, which we call religion. It was created not out of nothing but largely by the effective consolidation of the purely illusory aspect of primitive magic. Thus came into being a whole host of goddesses and gods, to whom the deliberate offering of the social surplus was not merely an act of piety but moreover supposed to ensure to the direct producers safety from various frightening calamities. To the direct producers themselves, such goddesses and gods were of course supposed to have substantive entities. Nevertheless, they also needed mundane or earthly representatives to act on their behalf and manage their affairs. Along with them, therefore, came into the social scene the class of priestesses and priests, who alone knew the secret of acting on their behalf. Such in brief is the account of the making of religion or its coming into being.

But it is also the account of the beginnings of class society. The social surplus accumulated in the city centres was not equally distributed among the actual workers (the farmers and full-time specialist craftsmen) and the priests and merchants etc., the latter forming the leisured class. It was not yet fully parasitical, inasmuch as its members remained as the organisers of production. But the organisers of production soon converted themselves into the owners of the means of production, and thus society was split into an owning class and a working class.

On archaeological evidence we now know that all this first took place about five thousand years ago in what Gordon Childe calls the three "primary centres" of the urban revolution, namely Egypt, Mesopotamia and the Indus Valley. Since then civilisation spread out practically all over the globe, though without disturbing the basic class structure of society, and, along with it, its ideological concomitant viz. religion, notwithstanding the circumstance of both class society and religion undergoing various changes within the general structure. Throughout this period, however, religion—though without foregoing its original function of extracting the surplus product of the direct producers—served also the purpose of offering consolation for avoidable miseries, or, as we have put it, providing with palliative remedies for these.

With these points in mind, we may now pass on to discuss the question we propose specially to discuss in the present lecture, namely the future of religion.

2. Class Society and its Future

As the making of religion is historically and necessarily connected with the making of class society, it is only logical for us to begin with some idea of the future of class society before passing on to the question of the future of religion. During the career of about five thousand years of civilisation the class structure of society underwent successive changes, until it assumed the form of modern capitalism. During these five thousand years, again, the technique of production underwent quantitative improvements, which assumed a qualitatively new form, as it were, under capitalism, so much so that it became basically incompatible with the class structure of society as such. Hence is the crisis in our times. Man is confronted with two irreconcilable alternatives. One of these is the abolition of the class structure of society. The other is to allow the productive technique to stagnate, or, if allowed to develop at all, developing mainly for destructive purpose or war—localised and even global. Imperialist countries have gone in for the second alternative. A brief but vivid idea of the real horror of this can be found in such fully documented books as *Monopoly Capital* by Baran and Sweezy.

What is greatly patronised by Imperialism as "social science" is often nothing but a screen to hide the ugliness of all this. But this is often torn to shreds by direct experience of the people. As Baran and Sweezy observe: "that idle men and idle machines coexist with deprivation at home and starvation abroad, that poverty grows in step with affluence, that enormous amounts of resources are wasted in frivolous and often harmful ways, that the United States has become the symbol and defender of reaction all over the world, that we are engaged in several wars and clearly headed towards more and bigger ones—the knowledge of all this, and much more, did not come to us from the social sciences but from the observation of unavoidable facts."[1]

The main point explained by the authors is quite simple. Monopoly capital is ultimately dominated by one motivation and that is maximum profit of the owners of the means of production and maximum profit is there in making or producing the weapons of destruction. As J.D. Bernal sums up: "It is the same demand for maximum profit that has given, in recent years, the heavy bias of technology and science towards military uses. Profits there are enormous: the public pays without asking awkward questions, and the resulting goods do not clog the market. They can be expended in wars or, if that fails, scrapped in a few years as obsolete. The demand for them is also reinforced by every means of propaganda needed to keep up war fever and justify military expenditure. One consequence of this has been the militarisation of science, with all its consequence of secrecy, screening and witch-hunting."[2]

All this gives us some idea of how the desperate attempts to preserve the class structure of society is wanting to misuse the tremendous technological developments of man: the knowledge of and power over nature acquired by man is threatening his very existence. As a result, there has grown the tendency in a certain section of thinkers to censure the technological development itself, its usual argument being that the lop-sided emphasis on material power and prosperity has undermined the spiritual upliftment of man, pushing him back to some new form of barbarism. Others with deeper insight into history and the laws of its development can see where the crisis actually belongs. It is not in the mastery over nature but in the class structure of society itself. Morgan's judgement (already quoted by us) pronounced over a hundred years back sounds prophetic today:

"A mere property career is not the final destiny of mankind, if progress is to be the law of the future as it has been of the past..... the dissolution of society bids fair to become the termination of a career of which property is the end and aim, because such a career contains the elements of self-destruction". Morgan said this depending mainly on the study of ancient society, but we have in the writings of Marx and Engels a very positive vision of human freedom resulting from the technological developments upto their times—a vision which enables us to understand the present and foresee the future. We quote Engels's lucid exposition of this from his *Socialism: Utopian and Scientific:*[3]

> Active social forces work exactly like natural forces: blindly, forcibly, destructively, so long as we do not understand and reckon with them. But when once we understand them, when once we grasp their action, their direction, their effects, it depends only upon ourselves to subject them more and more to our own will, and by means of them to reach our own ends. And this holds quite especially true of the mighty productive forces of today. As long as we obstinately refuse to understand the nature and the character of these social means of action, ...so long as these forces are at work in spite of us, in opposition to us, so long they master us....But when once their nature is understood, they can, in the hands of the producers working together, be transformed from master demons into willing servants. The difference is as that between the destructive force of electricity in the lightning of the storm, and the electricity under command in the telegraph and the voltaic arc: the difference between a conflagration, and fire working in the service of man.

How, then, are the working men and women going to use the knowledge of social forces and thereby attain mastery over these? The crucial point about it, as discovered by Marx and Engels, transformed socialism from the dream of the earlier utopians into an exact science. As Engels continued:

> With this recognition, at last, of the real nature of the productive forces of today, the social anarchy of production gives place to

> social regulation of production upon a definite plan, according to the needs of the community and of each individual. Then the capitalist mode of appropriation, in which the product enslaves first the producer and then the appropriator, is replaced by the mode of appropriation of the products that is based upon the nature of the modern means of production; upon the one hand, direct social appropriation, as means to the maintenance and extension of production—on the other, direct individual appropriation, as means of subsistence and of enjoyment. Whilst the capitalist mode of production more and more completely transforms the great majority of the population into proletarians, it creates the power which, under penalty of its own destruction, is forced to accomplish this revolution. Whilst it forces on more and more transformation of the vast means of production, already socialised, into state property, it shows itself the way to accomplishing this revolution. The proletariat seizes political power and turns the means of production into state property.

Social intervention thus based upon definite knowledge of social forces opens before man a new horizon of freedom. Here is the inspiring description of it given by Engels:

> With the seizing of the means of production by society, production of commodities is done away with, and, simultaneously, the mastery of the product over the producer. Anarchy in social production is replaced by systematic definite organisation. The struggle for individual existence disappears. Then for the first time man, in a certain sense, is finally marked off from the rest of the animal kingdom, and emerges from mere animal conditions of existence into really human ones. The whole sphere of the conditions of life which environ man, and which have hitherto ruled man, now comes under the dominion and control of man, who for the first time becomes the real conscious lord of Nature, because he has now become master of his own social organisation. The laws of his own social action hitherto standing face to face with man as laws of Nature foreign to and dominating him, will then be used with full understanding, and so mastered by him. Man's own social organisation, hitherto confronting him as a necessity imposed by Nature and history, now becomes the result of his own free

> action. The extraneous objective forces that have hitherto governed history pass under the control of man himself. Only from that time will man himself, more and more consciously make his own history—only from that time will the social causes set in movement by him have, in the main and in a constantly growing measure, the results intended by him. It is the ascent of man from the kingdom of necessity to the kingdom of freedom.

Such, then, is classless society or communism as understood in Marxism. It is only another world for conditions where men consciously make their own history. It is the human march forward from the realm of necessity to that of freedom.

3. Future of Religion

With this brief idea of the future of the class structure of society, we may now turn to our main problem, namely that of the future of religion.

Like the basic idea of communism, the condemnation of religion as a force wanting to keep the masses submissive to the privileged classes of society can be traced to a period much earlier than that of Marx and Engels. We shall begin with one example of this, specially because it expresses the ideas and attitudes not of the atheists and materialists but of very devout religious peoples. In books of European history they are mentioned as The Diggers. "In April 1649 about 20 poor men assembled at St. George's Hill, Surrey, and began to cultivate the common land. They held that the English Civil War had been fought against the King and the great landowners; now that Charles I had been executed, land should be made available for the very poor to cultivate". The number of the Diggers soon swelled up and their leader Gerrard Winstanley, himself a very pious Christian, came out with the most passionate denunciation of organised religion, when their movement was brutally suppressed and Winstanley was forced by bitter experience to recognise that 'organised' religion was in practice used "to reconcile the poor to their poverty by pretending to them that it was the will of God." As he put it,

> This Divining Doctrine, which you call spiritual and heavenly things, is the thief and robber that comes to spoil the vineyard of a man's peace, and does not enter at the door, but climbs up another way.... This divining spiritual doctrine is a cheat; for while men are gazing up to heaven, imagining after-happiness or fearing a hell after they are dead, their eyes are put out and they see not what is their birthright, and what is to be done by them here on earth while they are living. This is the filthy dreamer and the cloud without rain. And indeed the subtle clergy do know that if they can but charm the people by their divining doctrine to look after heavenly riches and glory after they are dead, then they shall easily be the inheritors of the earth and have the deceived people to be their servants.[4]

Winstanley, being himself a peasant after all, had neither the ability nor the taste for any sophisticated theoretical criticism of religion. But the view that "all religions, including Christianity too, were the work of deceivers"—a view that generally dominated the "free thinkers"—that religion "was no longer sufficient after Hegel who had set philosophy the task of showing a rational evolution in world history."[5] Hence, specially in Germany where the philosophers were greatly under the spell of Hegel, there came into being a flourishing literature produced by the angry young philosophers or radical thinkers showing the tendency to expose and criticise religion in sophisticated philosophical terms. This group of thinkers is generally referred to as the Young Hegelians who were the immediate predecessors of Marx. Marx himself, evidently because of his own radical bend of mind, was drawn into their movement and, even in his student days, became one of its most fiery leaders. But the alliance was not long to last. He started seeing the criticism of religion by the Young Hegelians—however passionate it might have been—had on the whole some kind of political romanticism and hence ineffective in the matter of uprooting religion. In fact, no amount of savage onslaught on religion could be the right way of fighting it. Already in 1842, he wrote to Ruge, about the Young Hegelians: "I asked them to criticise religion by criticising political conditions rather than the other way about, because religion, quite empty in itself, lives from earth and not from heaven and will disappear on its own once the inverted reality whose theory it represents is dissolved.[6]

This gives us some indication of the new turn Marx's thought was taking, which, as fully formed, found its first comprehensive expression in the book *German Ideology* drafted jointly by Marx and Engels. The decisive point of their departure from the Young Hegelians took place when they arrived at what is called the materialist conception of history or, more simply, Historical Materialism. Since the future of religion as visualised in Marxism—which as far as I understand, is the most scientific visualisation we have so far—follows from it, we may as well begin with a brief idea of it. Since Marxism is best understood in the words of Marx and Engels themselves, we quote here from the *German Ideology* at some length to see what they actually mean by Historical Materialism:

> The production of ideas, of conceptions, of consciousness, is at first directly interwoven with the material activity and the material intercourse of man, the language of real life. Conceiving and thinking, the mental intercourse of men, appear at this stage as the direct efflux of their material behaviour. The same applies to mental production as expressed in the language of politics, laws, morality, religion, metaphysics, etc., of a people. Men are the producers of their conceptions, ideas, etc.,—real, active men, as they are conditioned by a definite development of their productive forces and of the intercourse corresponding to these, up to its furthest forms. Consciousness can never be anything else than conscious existence, and the existence of men is their actual life-process. If in all ideology men and their circumstances appear upside-down as in a camera obscura, this phenomenon arises just as much from their historical life-process as the inversion of objects on the retina does from their physical life-process.

"In direct contrast to German philosophy which descends from heaven to earth, here we ascend from earth to heaven. That is to say, we do not set out from what men say, imagine, conceive, nor from men as narrated, thought of, imagined, conceived, in order to arrive at man in the flesh. We set out from real, active men, and on the basis of their real life-process we demonstrate the development of the ideological reflexes and echoes of their life-process. The phantoms formed in the human brain are also, necessarily, sublimates of their material life-process, which is empirically verifiable and bound to material premises. Morality, religion, metaphysics, all the rest of ideology and their corresponding forms of consciousness, thus no longer retain the semblance of independence. They have no history, no development; but men, developing their material production and their material intercourse, alter, along with this their real existence, their thinking and the products of their thinking. Life is not determined by consciousness, but consciousness by life. In the first method of approach the starting-point is consciousness taken as the living individual; in the second method, which conforms to real life, it is the real living individuals themselves, and consciousness is considered solely as their consciousness.[7]

Thus the philosophical views and in fact all ideological productions are, according to the Marxist analysis, ultimately conditioned by the material factors, namely the technique or mode of production and the relations of production resulting from it. It follows, therefore, that without a revolutionary transformation of these material conditions, there can be no revolutionary transformation in philosophical thought. Already in the *German Ideology*, Marx and Engels emphasised this. As they observe:

It [i.e. the materialistic conception of history] has not, like the idealistic view of history, in every period to look for a category, but remains constantly on the real ground of history; it does not explain practice from the idea but explains the formation of ideas form material practice; and accordingly it comes to the conclusion that all forms and products of consciousness cannot be dissolved by mental criticism.... but only by the

> practical overthrow of the actual social relations which gave rise to their idealistic humbug; that not criticism but revolution is the driving force of history, also of religion, philosophy and all other types of theory.[8]

To this is immediately to be added another point. Marx and Engels wanted repeatedly to draw our attention to the fact that there was something about the class structure of society as such which wanted to coerce the philosophers' consciousness to succumb to some basic illusion, without the philosophers themselves being aware of it. Therefore, the real emancipation of philosophy, as understood in Marxism, presupposes the revolutionary transformation of class society into classless society.

Already in the *Communist Manifesto*, they observe: "Does it require deep intuition to comprehend that man's ideas, views and conceptions, in one word, man's consciousness, changes with every change in the conditions of his material existence, in his social relations and in his social life?....

> ....The history of all past society has consisted in the development of class antagonisms that assumed different forms at different epochs.
>
> But whatever form they may have taken, one fact is common to all past ages, viz. the exploitation of one part of society by the other. No wonder, then, that the social consciousness of past ages, despite all the multiplicity and variety it displays, moves within certain common forms, or general ideas, which cannot completely vanish except with the total disappearance of class antagonisms.
>
> The communist revolution is the most radical rupture with traditional property relations; no wonder that its development involves the most radical rupture with traditional ideas.[9]

We can thus understand why in the Marxist understanding social revolution has an exceedingly important place even in the philosophical agenda. Without establishing the classless society, there is no effective emancipation of philosophy from the age-old illusions originating from the class structure of society itself. It is therefore imperative for the philosopher to change the world, and this even for the sake of philosophical emancipation. Hence is Marx's emphasis on *changing* the world, rather than remain satisfied merely with various attempts to understand it.

But all this is not to be misunderstood, and, in order not to misunderstand, the problem of relation between philosophical emancipation and social revolution is to be approached from the dialectical point of view.

From the dialectical point of view, consciousness—inclusive obviously of religious and philosophical consciousness—though ultimately rooted in material conditions, also reacts back on the material conditions. Consciousness, in other words, has also an active role. On this point, the founders of Marxism parted company with their materialist predecessors, who were on the whole taking a mechanical view of the environment conditioning our consciousness. As Marx very cryptically said in the *Third Thesis on Feuerbach:*

> The materialist doctrine that men are products of circumstances and upbringing, and that, therefore, changed men and products of other circumstances and changed upbringing, forgets that it is men that change circumstances and that the educator himself needs education....[10]

In Marxist understanding, thus, philosophers or theoreticians are not to await passively for the momentous social transformation to take place for the emancipation of their thought. For in the meanwhile there is something exceedingly important for them to do, which, though expected to be done in the special capacity of theoreticians or philosophers, is relevant for the social revolution. The most important thing is to change the world no doubt, but the point also is that there is no right way of changing the world with a wrong or inadequate understanding of it.

With these points in mind, let us turn to the question of how the essence as well as the future of religion is understood in Marxism. One of the best and most lucid expressions of this is found in the concluding chapter of Engels's *Anti-*

Dühring. We propose to wind up our lecture with an extract from it. Engels observed:

> All religion is nothing but the fantastic reflection in men's minds of those external forces which control their daily life, a reflection in which the terrestrial forces assume the form of supernatural forces. In the beginnings of history it was the forces of nature which were at first so reflected, and in the course of further evolution they underwent the most manifold and varied personifications among the various peoples..... But it is not long before, side by side with the forces of nature, social forces begin to be active; forces which present themselves to man as equally extraneous and at first equally inexplicable, dominating them with the same apparent necessity as the forces of nature themselves. The fantastic personifications, which at first only reflected the mysterious forces of nature, at this point acquire social attributes, become representatives of the forces of history. At a still further stage of evolution, all the natural and social attributes of the innumerable gods are transferred to one almighty god, who himself once more is only the reflex of the abstract man. Such was the origin of monotheism, which was historically the last product of the vulgarised philosophy of the later Greeks and found its incarnation in the exclusively national god of the Jews, Jehovah. In this convenient, handy and readily adaptable form religion can continue to exist as the immediate—that is, the sentimental—form of men's relation to the extraneous natural and social forces which dominate them, so long as men remain under the control of those forces. We have already seen, more than once, that in existing bourgeois society men are dominated by the economic conditions created by themselves, by the means of production which they themselves have produced, as if by an extraneous force. The actual basis of religious reflex action therefore continues to exist, and with it the religious reflex itself. And though bourgeois politcal economy has given a certain insight into the casual basis of this domination by extraneous forces, this makes no essential difference. Bourgeois economics can neither prevent crises in general, nor protect the individual capitalists from losses, bad debts and bankruptcy, nor secure the individual workers against unemployment and destitution.

> It is still true that man proposes and God (that is, the extraneous force of the capitalist mode of production) disposes. Mere knowledge, even if it went much further and deeper than that of bourgeois economic science, is not enough to bring social forces under the control of society. What is above all necessary for this is a social act. And when this act has been accomplished, when society, by taking possession of all means of production and using them on a planned basis, has freed itself and all its members from the bondage in which they are at present held by these means of production which they themselves have produced but which now confront them as an irresistible extraneous force; when therefore man no longer merely proposes but also disposes—only then will the last extraneous force which is still reflected in religion vanish; and with it will also vanish the religious reflection itself, for the simple reason that there will then be nothing left to reflect.[11]

To sum up: Religion was brought into being by the class structure of society; throughout the period of the class society religion drew its nourishment therefrom; with the active overthrow of the class structure of society, religion is destined to wither away. Religion, therefore, has no future—no more than the class society itself. In the absolute time-scale, however, class society is no more than a mere twinkling of the eye compared to the general history of the existence of human beings on the earth. So also is the life-span of religion.

"Ah! Faustus, now hast thou but one bare hour to live!"

REFERENCES

1. P.A. Baran & P.M. Sweezy 1-2.
2. J.D. Bernal iv. 1254.
3. K. Marx & F. Engels SW (Moscow 1975 edn.) 423-26.
4. Quoted by G. Thomson ER 20.
5. Engels in OR 193.
6. Marx to Ruge, Nov. 1842.
7. K. Marx & F. Engels GI 37-38.
8. *Ib.* 50.
9. K. Marx & F. Engels SW (Moscow 1977 ed). i. 125-26.
10. K. Marx TF *III*.
11. F. Engels AD 374-5.

Bibliography

ACI: *Ancient Cities of the Indus*, ed. Possehl G.L., New Delhi 1979

Agrawal, D.P. *Archaeology of India*, Copenhegen 1982

Allchin, B. & R. *The Birth of Indian Civilization*, Penguin 1968

Rise of Civilization in India and Pakistan, New Delhi 1983

Baran, P.A. & Sweezy, P.M. *Monopoly Capital*, New York 1966

Bernal, J.D. *Science in History*, Penguin 1969 edn.

Chattopadhyaya, D. *Lokayata*, New Delhi 1978 edn.

What is Living and What is Dead in Indian Philosophy, New Delhi 1976 edn.

Childe, V. Gordon *Man Makes Himself*, London 1951 ed.

New Light on the Most Ancient East, New York 1954 ed.

What Happened in History, 1957 ed.

The Urban Revolution (reprint in ACI)

de Bary, W.T. (ed.) *Sources of Indian Tradition*, New York 1958

Dunham, B. *Heroes and Heretics*, New York 1967

EIP: *Essays in Indian Proto-history*, ed D.K. Chakrabarti and D.P. Agrawal, New Delhi 1979

Engels, F. *Anti-Dühring*, Moscow 1947 edn.

Origin of Family, Private Property and the State, Moscow 1952 edn.

ERE: *Encyclopaedia of Religion and Ethics*

FIC: *Frontiers of the Indus Civilization*, ed. B.B. Lal and S.P. Gupta, Delhi 1984

Freud, S. *The Future of an Illusion*, Pelican Freud Library, Vol. 12

Ghosh, A. *The City in Early Historical India*, Simla 1973

Harrison, J.E. *Ancient Art and Ritual*, London 1935 ed.

IA: *Indian Antiquary*

Keith, A.B. *Karma-mīmāṃsā*, London 1921

Khaṇḍadeva, *Bhāṭṭa-dīpikā*

Kosambi, D.D. *An Introduction to the Study of Indian History*, Bombay 1956

Kumārila, *Śloka-vārtikā*
Macdonell, A.A. *Vedic Mythology*, Strassburg 1897
Marshall, J. *Mohenjodaro and the Indus Civilization*, London 1931
Marx, K. *Theses on Feuerbach*
Contribution to the Critique of Hegel's Philosophy of Right.
Marx, K. and Engels, F. *On Religion* (Selection), Moscow 1956
The German Ideology, Moscow 1964 ed.
Selected Works, Moscow 1975 ed.
Max Müller, F. *Collected Works*, Vol. XIX, London 1859
Mcrainu, B. *The Method and Theory of V. Gordon Childe*, Edinburgh 1980
Morgan, L.H. *Ancient Society*, Calcutta 1982 edn.
MS: *Mīmāṃsā-sūtra* of Jaimini
Needham, J. *The Grand Titration*, London 1979 ed.
Oldenberg, H. *Buddha: His Life, His Doctrine, His Order*, Calcutta 1927
Radhakrishnan, S. *Indian Philosophy*, Vol. I, London, 1923
Renou, L. *Religions of India*, London 1953
Rhys Davids, T.W.R. *Dialogues of the Buddha*, London Vol. I 1899, Vol. II 1910, Vol. III 1921
Ṛv: *Ṛgveda*
Sastri, H.P. *Haraprasāda Racanāvalī* (in Bengali), Calcutta, 1960
SBE: *Sacred Books of the East*
Sharma, R.S. *Material Culture and Social Formations in Ancient India*, New Delhi 1983
Stcherbatsky, Th. *Central Conception of Buddhism*, London 1923
Canception of Buddhist Nirvana, reprint Varanasi
Further Papers of Stcherbatsky, Calcutta 1971
Papers of Stcherbartsky, Calcutta 1969
Soul Theory of the Buddhists, reprint Varanasi 1970
Tanjur: *Catalogue of Indian Buddhist Texts in Tibetan Translation. Alphabetically Arranged* by A. Chattopadhyaya, Calcutta 1983
THBI: *Tārānātha's History of Buddhism in India*, Eng. Tr., Simla 1970
Thomson, G. *An Essay on Religion*, London 1950
Studies in Ancient Greek Society, London Vol. I 1949; Vol. II (*The First Philosophers)* 1955
Wheeler, R.E.M. *The Indus Civilization*, Cambridge 1979 ed.
Winternitz, M. *History of Indian Literature*, Calcutta Vol. I 1927, Vol. II 1933
Woolley, L. *History of Mankind: Culture and Scientific Development*, (Vol. I, Part 2) UNESCO 1963

Index